Raising Henry

Raising Henry

A Memoir of Motherhood, Disability, & Discovery

RACHEL ADAMS

Yale

UNIVERSITY PRESS

New Haven & London

Published with assistance from the foundation established in memory of Philip Hamilton McMillan of the Class of 1894, Yale College.

Frontispiece: The author and Henry. Photo by Heather Forbes.

Yale University Press books may be purchased in quantity for educational, business, or promotional use. For information, please e-mail sales.press@yale.edu (U.S. office) or sales@yaleup.co.uk (U.K. office).

Designed by Sonia Shannon.
Set in Fournier type by IDS Infotech Ltd.
Printed in the United States of America.

Library of Congress Cataloging-in-Publication Data

Adams, Rachel, 1968–. Raising Henry : a memoir of motherhood, disability, and discovery / Rachel Adams.
pages cm
Includes bibliographical references.
ISBN 978-0-300-18000-8 (cloth)
ISBN 978-0-300-19891-1 (paperback)
1. Adams, Rachel, 1968–.
2. Down syndrome—Patients—United States—Biography.
3. Developmentally disabled children—United States—Biography.
4. Parents of developmentally disabled children—United States—Biography. 5. Mothers and sons—United States—Biography. I. Title.
RJ506.D68A33 2013
618.92'8588420092—dc23
[B]
2013002096

A catalogue record for this book is available from the British Library.

Author's Note

THE BOOK THAT YOU ARE reading contains a true story. I have changed the names of some of the people involved out of respect for their privacy. The conversations in the book all come from my clear recollection of them, though they are not written to represent word-for-word transcripts. Rather, I have retold them in a way that evokes the feeling and meaning of what was said. In all instances, the essence of the dialogue is accurate.

The centrally exciting and important fact, from which ramify the thousand others which otherwise would have no clear and valid existence, is: that was the way it was. What could be more moving, more significant or true: every force and hidden chance in the universe has so combined that a certain thing was the way it was.

—James Agee, *Let Us Now Praise Famous Men*

Contents

Contents

Acknowledgments

MANY PARENTS OF A NEW BABY with Down syndrome have found solace in Emily Perl Kingsley's essay "Welcome to Holland." My road map was Michael Bérubé's book *Life as We Know It*. It taught me that having a child with Down syndrome was not a tragedy, and that it could, instead, become a route to profound personal and intellectual discovery. It helped me to welcome my son into our family and challenge the world to make a place for him. Thank you Michael, Janet, and Jamie for leading the way.

The worst thing about learning that our child had Down syndrome was the feeling of being utterly alone. I am grateful to all the people who showed me how wrong I was. Tracy Nixon, Rosemary Suh, Angela Watkins, Deirdre and John LaPolla, Ursula Hennessey, and Kate and Ray Schaub were there at the beginning. So was Jordana Mendelson, who astonishes me with her strength, resilience, and optimism. These parents were joined by Dena Chase Wenner, Jane and Anthony Providenti, Debbie and Andrew Morris, Susan Heim, Cindy Chao, Stacey Calcano, Margie Rosado, Britt Sady, and so many others. During Henry's early life, we were also sustained by the Bank

Street Family Center Parent-Toddler Group, which included Lucinda Rosso, Stephanie Perlman, Elaina LaRusso, Ann Hairston, Lara Gerstein, and Bruce and Abby Levine. George Estreich and Alison Piepmeier have offered wisdom and inspiration from afar. Sara Pines, Jenny Eisenberg, and Victoria Rosner have been the best of friends.

A sentence is hardly enough to record our gratitude to the many wonderful educators and therapists who have worked with Henry over the years. Among them, our first, brilliant EI team—Gay Rosenberg, Munira Adenwalla, Denise Colina, and Marquis English— deserves special mention, as do the wise and loving teachers at the Bank Street Family Center and Central Park Early Learning Center. Sarah Lee, our kind and dedicated EI service coordinator, helped us to find our way. Dr. Herb Lazarus has been the best pediatrician we could ever hope for. My deepest thanks go to Angela Grullón, who allows me to go to work confident that Henry will be loved and cared for.

Henry has rocked my intellectual world, and I am grateful to the many people who helped me take my work in new directions. Narrative medicine opened my eyes to the power of storytelling, and I thank Rita Charon, Maura Spiegel, Marsha Hurst, and Sayantani DasGupta for letting me learn from them. Marsha Hurst and Sayantani DasGupta's Narrative Genetics seminar was especially important as I began to think about the intellectual implications of having a person with a disability in my family. I am grateful to colleagues in disability studies who let me back in after many years when I had turned my attention elsewhere. Of particular importance is the work of Rosemarie Garland-Thomson, Tobin Siebers, Michael Bérubé, Susan Schweik, Michael Davidson, Faye Ginsburg, Eva Feder Kittay, Rayna Rapp, and Lennard Davis. The Future of Disability Studies project that I direct at Columbia could not exist without the enthusiastic participation of colleagues from around the region, and I thank the Center for the Study of Social Difference for sponsoring us. Other colleagues who supported me during the writing of this book include Jean Howard, Jenny Davidson, Julie Crawford, Monica Miller, Elizabeth Leake, Debbie Ashe, Marianne Hirsch, Alondra Nelson, Chris Brown, and Hilary Hallett. Of this group Liz Emens, Victoria Rosner, and Maura Spiegel have been exceptional friends and colleagues.

This book represents an attempt to reinvent myself as a writer, and my earliest efforts were enabled by the encouragement of Charles Salzberg's writing group. Thanks to Lindsey Wickhoff, Amy Flynn, Amy Dombro, and Ellen Galinsky for answering questions that helped me to understand Bank Street as an institution. Mary Miller and Caroline Lieber gave me opportunities to talk about genetics and pregnancy. To my former agent, the irrepressible Priscilla Gilman, thank you for seeing the possibilities in this book and finding someone who would publish it. I am grateful to Alison MacKeen at Yale University Press for embracing my project and to Jean Thomson Black for taking it on in her absence. Thanks to Dan Heaton for his able and affirming copyediting.

This is partly a story about loss, and, much as my writing has benefited from the presence of supportive colleagues, friends, and family, it has also been informed by memories of those who aren't there to experience it. My life as a parent is colored by the loss of my mother, Ruth Lauren Adams, whose absence also gave shape to this story. I mourn the loss of Peggy Sradnick, who embraced Henry as she did all the other children she welcomed into the Basic Trust. My godmother Diane Kovacs blazed the way, and I wish she were here to share Henry's story with me.

Without my family this book could not exist. I thank them for giving me something important to write about, if not always the time to write. HuEllen and Bill have been the most loving grandparents I could ever imagine. Sam and Kathy encouraged my attempts to be a different kind of writer. Olivia allowed herself to be written about. Naomi, whom I think of as my other sister, gave me insight about growing up with a disabled brother. My beloved Noah and Henry are the reason for it all. Their many demands and temptations make it hard to find time and mental energy to write. But they also give writing a sense of urgency and purpose. When Jon Connolly first read this manuscript he commented on how small a part I had given him in our story. I try to remind him, in my own imperfect way, that if he isn't on every page, his wisdom, generosity, and kindness are behind them all.

Raising Henry

Prelude

IN THE PICTURE WE'RE DANCING. He's slightly out of focus, illuminated by a sunbeam coming in from the window. His expression is pure delight. I'm off to the side, my face in shadow. But I'm smiling too as I hold him tightly with one arm. The other arm is outstretched, our hands clasped as I lead him in this joyful dance.

This is my favorite picture of Henry and me. It was taken by Heather, the pricey child photographer we hired after seeing her work in a local magazine. When we got the proofs, each more beautiful than the one before, I found it hard to restrain myself, and suddenly I had run up a jaw-dropping bill. It's an expensive habit, and I always promise that each time will be our last. Then spring comes around and I realize that, once again, nobody has taken a single picture of me since the last time we saw Heather. In her absence, I'm the family photographer, and if I want pictures, I have to take them. The person taking the pictures can't also be in them. I wonder how I'll be remembered if there aren't any pictures.

I remember my mother only through pictures. I have plenty to choose from since my father was an incessant documentarian of our family life. Two black-and-white photographs hang in the hall between the living room and the kitchen. In one, she's sitting outside, playing the *viola da gamba*, a baroque cello whose neck ends in the carved bust of a woman. She wears a long black dress, her dark hair swept into an elegant bun, head bowed with concentration. Serious and composed, the face of the instrument mirrors the face of my mother. In the other, my parents pose smiling by the gangway of a plane bound for Japan. Those were the days when people dressed for travel. She's wearing a dark tailored suit. He's in pressed jeans, striped tie, and a trench coat. They make an especially glamorous and attractive couple. I keep another picture of my mother in a box in my closet. I know she's exactly my age because she was already dying. She's lying in bed, her hair still dark and thick but cut short because she was no longer able to take care of it. I wonder what she was thinking as she smiled for the camera, knowing that she might not be there to see the film developed.

PART ONE

Arrival

THERE ARE NO PHOTOGRAPHS OF that day in the labor and delivery room where I first held my new son. When his older brother, Noah, was born, I'd started taking pictures the minute I could sit up, finding his scrawny limbs and misshapen red face indescribably beautiful. Henry had the same scaly newborn feet and shock of dark hair, but there was something about him that didn't quite make sense to me. Or perhaps I knew all too well what I was seeing. And neither my husband, Jon, nor I had made any move to pick up the camera.

I felt a tremendous sense of calm. This, after the bright lights, the shouts of doctors and nurses, pricking needles, hands groping roughly inside of me, the primordial screams of some other woman—but it must have been me—a searing pain, the hot, liquid gush of birth, the sharper more localized pain of being stitched back together. The resident who presided over the birth was an implausibly young man I had never seen before. When it was over, he spent half an hour between my legs, repairing the most intimate parts of my body. The birth had happened so fast he said the tearing was like "road burn," hard to sew up but quick to heal. He finished what he was doing and stepped back to survey his work. Concluding that it was good enough, he told me the stitches would fall out within a few weeks and left the room.

He must have known, but he didn't show it. He didn't say anything about it to me, and I never saw him again. I guess he thought his work was done once the baby was delivered. Breaking the news would be someone else's job.

IN THE STILLNESS THAT followed, a nurse kept moving the baby to different positions, trying to get him to latch on to my breast. His mouth opened and closed weakly. No sound came out. The room was completely quiet and filled with watery winter sunlight.

A pediatrician arrived. She introduced herself and told us she was going to examine our baby. She spread him on a heated table and turned her back. A few minutes later, she wrapped him up and handed him back to me.

"I was called here because your baby has features consistent with Down syndrome," she said. "He's pink and he looks healthy, but we're going to have to take him back to the NICU, the neonatal intensive care unit, and run some tests to make sure his heart is functioning properly."

The world should have stopped.

"I know this is a lot to take in. Do you have any questions for me?"

Of course I had questions. *Couldn't you give me just a few more minutes to imagine that my baby is perfect? Isn't every parent entitled to believe that anything is possible for her new child? Why were you in such a hurry to snatch away my fantasy? How could this be happening?*

I shook my head.

"I'll be back later and we can talk more then," she said kindly. She let Jon hold our baby for a few minutes. Then she placed him in a wheeled cart and pushed him out of the room.

After she left, the room was still quiet and sunny. I still felt calm. Somewhere beneath the surface, I knew that fear, grief, and rage were roiling. But I was wrapped in a numbing blanket of hormones that invited my body to relax even as my mind started to race.

Once the doctor was gone, I looked to Jon to tell me how to feel. Jon had always supplied the emotional ballast in our relationship. He is sensible and contemplative where I'm reactive and volatile. He had read every word I had ever written, marking the pages with comments and patiently enduring my frustration when I couldn't find a way to express the arguments piling up in my head. I dedicated my first book to Jon, my best editor and my best friend.

When we found each other in graduate school, neither of us could quite believe our good fortune. We marveled at the coincidences that caused our very different lives to intersect. I grew up in a woodsy bungalow in the canyons of Los Angeles, surrounded by my parents' bohemian circle of musicians and artists. There were chamber music concerts in our living room. We took weekend camping trips where everyone went skinny-dipping together. My mother drove a VW bus with flowers painted on the side. Jon came from a small suburb in Georgia where there was a church on almost every corner. His father's parents were Appalachian tobacco farmers, and his mother didn't have an indoor toilet until she was a teenager. Everybody in town was white and Christian, and everybody knew everybody else. What Jon and I had in common were our memories of being lonely, painfully shy children who took refuge in books.

We fell in love while we were teaching assistants for a large lecture class on Shakespeare. We stared into each other's eyes when the professor read love scenes from *Twelfth Night*. I lent Jon a copy of A. S. Byatt's novel *Possession*, about a couple of geeky academics who discover evidence of a secret romance between two Victorian poets. Jon invited me to go with him to a weekend conference on Renaissance literature, which seemed like the most romantic getaway I could imagine. Our scribbled notes quickly evolved from sarcastic jokes to heated expressions of desire. The students, who were only a few years younger than we, could see exactly what was going on. Knowing that they were spying on us made our flirtations all the more exciting. We did everything together. We had the same friends and the same interests, and we earned the same pathetically small graduate stipend. Our love was awkward and bookish, and we both quickly decided it was forever.

Thirteen years later, we lived on the opposite end of the country. We had careers and a mortgage. Becoming parents threatened the perfect equality that was so important to how we understood ourselves as a unit. Reality sunk in on the Monday morning after Noah was born, when Jon got out of bed, showered, and put on his suit. He was an associate at a large law firm, his completed dissertation packed away in some forgotten corner of our apartment. The partners had sent an enormous basket of gifts for our new baby, along with plenty of email to remind Jon of everything he needed to do when he got back to the office. I knew he had to go to work, but somehow I couldn't believe it was happening until the door clicked shut behind him. I sat there holding Noah, stunned by the realization that I was a mother, which meant that I would be left alone to care for this strange baby wriggling in my arms and threatening to cry.

I disliked staying home with my baby, and I hated myself for disliking it. The other moms I met apparently had more tolerance for the discomfort and boredom of having an infant than I did. Some of them even seemed to be enjoying themselves. I found myself wishing I had a mother of my own to prepare me for what to expect or to validate my feelings. Maybe, I thought when I felt most sorry for myself, women who had themselves been mothered possessed some emotional reserve that I lacked. Maybe on some unconscious level they remembered being cared for, and that made it easier to accept the selflessness required of a new mother. Whatever the reason, I took little pleasure in pushing the stroller around our neighborhood, the endless rounds of feeding and diapering, and long afternoons trying to keep baby Noah entertained. Suddenly Jon and I found ourselves living out the most clichéd battles of modern parenthood. I was desperate to get back to work, and I resented him for leaving me at home with the baby. All he wanted was time at home with the baby. He was irritated by my complaints. I was the one who had the flexible job as a tenured professor, with the generous parental leave that allowed me to take off an entire semester at full pay. The problem was that I didn't earn nearly enough to cover our expenses, meaning that we relied on Jon's salary to pay the bills. We were snappish and impatient with each other, and our arguments sounded tired, like the echoes of arguments taking place in hundreds of thousands of other households everywhere around us.

Despite all of this, we were completely besotted with our new baby. Whatever hardship parenting had brought to our lives was more than outweighed by the joy we found in Noah, who, we decided, was the most beautiful, charming, and perfect human ever to be born. We recorded his every experience with snapshots, home videos, and copious notes for his baby book. I saved everything: the tiny plastic ankle bracelet he wore in the hospital, his first nail clippings, the first hairs cut from his head, first shoes, socks, sweater, finger-, hand-, and footprints. We obsessed and hovered, afraid we might miss something. We competed for his attention, each wanting to be the one who made him laugh loudest or the one he reached for when he was upset. At night we compared notes, rehearsing all of the miraculous things Noah had done during the day. Before long, we started to wonder what Noah's future brother or sister might be like. We loved him so much, it seemed unthinkable that we would never know this hypothetical sibling who, we imagined, would be just as marvelous and as perfect as his big brother.

JON HEARD WHAT THE DOCTOR had said about Henry, and he wasn't crying. He gazed at our new son with the same look of wonder and curiosity that I remembered from his first pictures with Noah. He held Henry just as gently. The finger that caressed Henry's cheek was no less loving than it had been for our first baby. I looked at Jon looking at Henry and tried to draw from his strength. It helped that, regardless of what my mind was thinking, the hormones kept my body in a state of euphoric relaxation.

My hormonal calm had vanished by the time I was settled in a grim little room in the maternity ward. Jon had gone home to take care of Noah, who, at twenty-two months, was little more than a baby himself. In the rooms around me other families were getting to know their new babies. Fathers walked the halls talking on cell phones. Visitors strolled by my open door carrying balloons and flowers. Nurses and orderlies bustled. It was Christmas Eve. The napkin that came with my gray meatloaf had a wreath on it.

Jon came back with Noah in tow. They'd had a terrible time getting to the hospital and it was late. The subway broke down and everyone had to get off. So Jon lugged Noah and his stroller onto a crowded bus that took them the rest of the way.

Arrival

Noah expressed brief interest in my pajamas, which were pink with donuts on them, and in the wheelchair I was supposed to use for getting around. Then he got impatient and it was time for them to leave. I felt a spasm of panic.

Jon handed me a white paper bag. "I brought you cake." His face fell. "Almost everything is closed. It's the only cake I could find. It's Christmas, and I don't want to leave you alone."

"It's okay," I lied. "You go home and take care of Noah. I'll be fine. I have to stay here with our baby."

After they left, I couldn't stop crying. I'd like to say I cried because I was worried about the baby upstairs in the NICU. But I didn't feel much of anything for him. I was mourning the loss of the son I thought I was going to have and the family I imagined we would be.

My Favorite Freak

FOR MY TWENTY-FIFTH BIRTHDAY, Jon gave me a book of Diane Arbus photographs, which he inscribed "for my favorite freak." He was alluding to my growing obsession with freak shows.

It began as my dissertation topic, but it quickly took on a life of its own that went far beyond the requirements of my academic research. I spent years in archives and libraries getting to know the great freaks of the past: Tom Thumb; The Missing Link, or What Is It?; the Siamese twins Chang and Eng; the giant Henry Wadlow; the Venus Hottentot; Jo-Jo the Dog-Faced Boy. I watched Tod Browning's classic film *Freaks* again and again. I was especially drawn to pictures of anonymous and long-forgotten people, a woman with three breasts, another with horns, a boy with the lower body of a half-formed twin brother emerging from his abdomen. I visited Coney Island and hipster freak shows in Williamsburg and on the Bowery. I spent one memorable Halloween at an art school in Baltimore, where I shared a panel on freaks with an aged showman and the surviving cast of the early John Waters films. I lay awake at night thinking about sideshows, only to fall asleep and find freaks peering at me solemnly in my dreams.

More than one person had written a history of the freak show. There were plenty of biographies of famous impresarios like P. T. Barnum and the Ringling Brothers. But I wanted to know about the freaks themselves, what they felt when people stared at them and what their lives were like when they weren't performing. I wrote and rewrote, trying to get their stories right. Eventually, miraculously and unexpectedly, the book about freaks got me tenure at Columbia University.

Although I hardly thought about having a baby until some years after the book was published, I was always interested in stories of pregnancy and monstrous births. Maybe it took me so long to want a child of my own because I knew just how seriously things could go wrong. Until well into the nineteenth century, it was widely believed that a pregnant woman had the power to imprint her experiences on the developing fetus. A mother-to-be longs for strawberries in December, and in June her baby is born with a strawberry-shaped birthmark. Sometimes, the powers of the maternal imagination were far more destructive. A woman named Ann E. Leak Thompson, born with no arms, traced her condition to the dark evening when her pregnant mother was surprised to see her abusive husband stumbling home drunk with a coat slung around his shoulders. It was said that Lionel the Lion-Faced Boy was covered in hair because his pregnant mother witnessed his father being mauled to death by a lion. Joseph Merrick, the Elephant Man, claimed that his mother was attacked by a circus elephant, leaving marks of the trauma on the surfaces of his body. I knew these stories weren't true, and I imagined the terrible burden carried by mothers who believed they were responsible for their children's suffering. But I was also intrigued by the idea of a maternal imagination so potent that it could influence the shape of a new life.

People were always asking what compelled me to write about freaks. I knew they thought my odd academic interests must be driven by some equally odd quirk in my past. They were hoping for a good story, and invariably I was a disappointment. I never knew how to answer them because I wasn't quite sure myself. It might have been the year my best friend Naomi and I found a copy of Leslie Fiedler's *Freaks: Myths and Images of the Secret Self* in our vacation house. We weren't very interested in the words, but we spent hours poring over the pictures of the hermaphrodite with breasts and a penis, fat men and ladies, two-headed babies, and the Elephant Man.

Or maybe it was the summer I discovered, to my horror, that I was growing a mustache and coarse hairs began to sprout from my chin. For years I did everything I could to get rid of them: plucking and tweezing, furtively shaving with my father's razor, burning my skin with waxes and depilatories. I finally met a mother-and-daughter team of electrologists and, after months of costly and painful treatments, the hair was gone. But no matter how smooth my face, I couldn't shake a lingering sense that somewhere inside of me lurked a bearded lady.

Or maybe I just identified with the freak's perpetual status as an outsider.

I don't actually believe any of this. What I really think is much crazier. It requires a willing suspension of traditional ideas about cause and effect. But humor me: I think I wrote that book to prepare me to be Henry's mother.

The Phantom Nephew

THEY OFFERED ME SLEEPING PILLS to get through that first night in the hospital. For the soreness, the nurse explained. The pain between my legs was nothing compared to the pain I felt when I thought about my new baby. I had spent much of my career probing the pain of misfits and outsiders. I had pored over their stories so deeply that at times their lives seemed more vivid than my own. I had sought meaning in the suffering of others. Now I wondered whether I had done something to make this baby what he was. Had I imprinted my obsession with deviance onto my son, whose difference was replicated in each of the millions of cells that made up his tiny body?

I knew these questions could lead to madness, but still I refused the drugs. I've never liked the feeling of being medicated. In college, I sometimes hung out with the Deadheads, thinking I might absorb some of their groovy equanimity. They embodied everything I wasn't. I admired their rejection of the kind of middle-class striving I had been taught to value, the way they could give themselves over to drugs and music as if nothing else mattered. I burned incense and dressed in Indian prints and tried to fit in. But I also liked to study and talk about books. I was a good student, who enjoyed my academic success. I wasn't willing to compromise it by writing my papers stoned or missing class to go to a concert. And the drugs made me nervous. I hated the feeling of being out of control.

After Henry was born, sleeping pills seemed like an easy escape, a way to avoid confronting the worry and fear that were already making my mind turn in circles.

As soon as I said no, I was sorry. Although I was exhausted, I lay in bed awake for hours before falling into a fitful sleep. I woke up repeatedly, looking around the half-dark of the hospital room in confusion until I remembered where I was. As I became conscious, the events of the past day would sink in and I would dissolve into tears. I cried until I was too tired to cry any more. Then I would fall back asleep, only to wake up oppressed by grief again.

At one point, I dreamed about my phantom nephew, who had been somewhere in the back of my mind all afternoon. He floated up out of darkness, bathed in the revealing yellow light of a medical photograph. There were slits of flesh where his eyes should be. He didn't have much of a nose, and in place of his mouth was a pinkish gap in the middle of his face. I waved at him and, as he waved back, I saw extra fingers sprouting limply from his wrist and the palm of his tiny hand.

The phantom nephew would have been a year older than Henry. I learned about him on a late-summer night after I had put Noah to bed. I was baking a cake and trying to enjoy the view from our kitchen window. At that time of year, sunsets on the Upper West Side can be stunning. I could hear laughter and live music wafting cheerily from a bar across the street. On evenings like this, I tried not to feel oppressed by thoughts of our crushing mortgage payments. Jon was working late as usual, missing so much in the life of the child we planned to raise together. I was reminded of how far we were from graduate school, when everything was equal. Nobody had any money and nobody owned anything and we thought that was the way it should be.

Once or twice a week, my sister Olivia would call while she drove home from work in Los Angeles and I was alone, cooking dinner in New York. That night her voice was halting and strange.

"I just talked to the doctor about my ultrasound," she said. "There are some problems."

"What kind of problems?"

"The baby. Its heart is too large, the head is too small, there's fluid where there shouldn't be." Her voice was shaking. "They told me that things just don't look right. Some of the organs aren't developing the way they're supposed to."

"What does that mean?" I knew I sounded impatient, but I couldn't help myself. Olivia was too trusting. She put too much stock in authority figures. And besides, I couldn't accept that what she was telling me could be true.

"I have to get rid of it."

"What do you mean?" I was shouting. "You don't know that. Of course you have to get a second opinion. What if the doctor is wrong?"

"He's not wrong," she said firmly. "It's not just the ultrasound. I got the results of the amnio today. It has Trisomy 13 and I have to get rid of it." She was almost five months pregnant, and had just endured several months of nausea and sweltering heat. "I guess the only good in this is that I know what I have to do. This thing might not survive until it's born. If it did, it would almost surely die soon after that. It's not like it could live and I have to decide whether I want it or not. There's no choice to be made."

I started to cry. "I just don't want it to be true." I was beating eggs furiously. "It's too sad. It shouldn't be true." I tried to collect myself. I knew I wasn't helping her by falling apart. I felt far away, aware that I was just starting a semester so busy I could hardly catch my breath. "What can I do? I wish I could be there."

"Can you call dad? I can't bear to tell him."

I talked to my father while I poured the batter and put the cake into the oven. Then I called some other close family friends. We were celebrating a neighbor's birthday later that weekend. When I ate my slice of cake, it tasted like sadness.

WHEN I GOT OFF THE PHONE, I sat down at my computer and started to research Trisomy 13. The images that my Google search turned up were unforgettable. A face with a hideously cleft palate and two misshapen black holes where eyes should be. Another with no eyes at all, a gaping, raw hole instead of a nose. One covered in brown fur, with a trunklike protrusion in the center of its face and a single, small slit for an eye. Hands with extra fingers and fingers missing. Bodies bent and twisted.

It turns out that ending a pregnancy in the twentieth week is not an easy thing to do. At the clinic, my visibly pregnant sister had to walk through protestors who shouted at her and waved signs saying CHOOSE LIFE! and ABORTION KILLS. One had a picture of a fetus in its amniotic bubble, as if it had floated free of the woman who carried it. Someone called Olivia a murderer. A woman in the waiting room sat too close and asked her what she was doing there. She wouldn't stop, even as Olivia cried softly and asked again and again to be left alone.

The procedure was complicated, and Olivia had to return to the clinic repeatedly, each time crossing the lines of hostile antiabortion protestors. First she was given an injection to stop the fetal heartbeat.

She went back to begin the process of cervical dilation, which took several days. The doctor explained that on her final visit she would be put under general anesthesia while the fetus was surgically removed.

She was supposed to have this stage of the procedure on a Wednesday morning. But, as with everything else in this pregnancy, all didn't go as planned.

I had just finished teaching and was walking back to my office when she called. I sat on a bench outside.

"Is it over?" I asked.

"They couldn't do it," she told me flatly. "After they put me to sleep they found I wasn't dilated enough. When I woke up they told me I'm still pregnant. I have to come back tomorrow and start all over again." Her voice broke. "I can't believe this is happening. I just want it to be over. I want it out of me." The early afternoon was sunny and warm. A group of students walked past, talking and joking. The dissonance between their carefree laughter and Olivia's misery was almost unbearable.

That night, her water broke and she developed a fever. Her husband drove her back to the clinic, where there was only one nurse on duty. She agreed to admit Olivia, but told him he wasn't allowed to stay. He sat outside in the car all night. While he was sleeping, my sister went into labor and delivered the fetus into the toilet. There was another woman sharing the room, their beds divided by a thin curtain. The bloody mass sat in the strainer hanging over the bowl until doctors could confirm what it was.

By the time this nightmare was over, she was so relieved that the sadness of losing the pregnancy had dissipated. "My doctor says we can try again in three months," she told me matter-of-factly. "Trisomy 13 isn't hereditary so I'll have the same chances—one in five thousand—as any other woman."

The Phantom Nephew

Four months later she was pregnant and the next fall she gave birth to a perfectly healthy baby boy named Owen.

When I saw pictures of my nephew, who was so delightfully chubby and pleasant, I couldn't help thinking of his older sibling. Although Olivia asked not to know the sex, I decided that he was a boy. I call him my phantom nephew, the one who wasn't meant to be.

Some women lose pregnancies too easily. My sister and I hung on to ours, each carrying a life that might have been rejected by another woman's body. I was six when our mother died. Olivia was just four. We remember so little about her. I wonder whether we cling to our own children because we know that life can be short and it is always unpredictable. Sometimes, I wince when I hear Olivia snap at her kids. Usually the offense seems pretty innocuous to me, whether it's kicking the back of the car seat, playing with their food, or whining. But then again, I recognize something of myself in her. It's not always pleasant to be the objects of our love. We are fierce and sometimes rough, desperate to leave a mark, determined to be remembered.

Learning Curve

HENRY SPENT THE FIRST DAYS of his life in the NICU, where doctors monitored his heart, his oxygen levels, and his feeding. One night our pediatrician, the kind and unflappable Dr. Zimmerman, stopped by the hospital on his way home from work. After listening carefully to Henry's heart, he turned his attention to us. Jon had developed an angry red sty on one eyelid. He hadn't shaved for days. I was wearing pajamas, my hair pulled back into a tangled ponytail. Neither of us had slept more than a few hours at a time since Henry had been born. We looked terrible.

"You're going to have a steep learning curve," he said gently, as he shook our hands goodbye.

Steep indeed.

We got started right away. What else was there for us to do? We were two people who had spent most of our lives with our heads in a book. When we weren't at the hospital, we read books and scoured the Internet to learn everything we could about Down syndrome. We found nothing useful in any of the prenatal guides stacked under my bedside table. I was struck by the fact that every one of them referred to the likelihood of conceiving a fetus with Down syndrome as a "risk," a word that implies a danger to be avoided. Because older women are more likely to conceive babies with Down syndrome, they explain, more extensive prenatal testing is recommended. To avoid risk. I thought about what difference it would make if they used the word "chance" instead. Few books bothered with any further explanation, as if it were unthinkable that a woman would venture beyond the discovery that her fetus was imperfect. Some of them raised the possibility of abortion, which, they implied, was the only viable option in the face of such unwelcome news.

One book went into more detail. It reported, "These children have an identifiable look with eyes that slant upwards and ears that fold over. They often have short necks, small noses, and small hands. Mental retardation can range from mild to serious." I found this description disturbing. It reminded me of eugenic theories from the early twentieth century, which described inferior classes of people by listing their physical features. The prevailing belief was that negative traits like criminality, low intelligence, and degeneracy could be read on the surfaces of the body. The word "retardation" felt like a slap in the face. I hadn't known people even used the word "retarded" anymore, except for the teenagers I heard shouting at each other on the subway during the after-school rush. "Dude, that's so retarded!" they would say to describe something impossibly stupid or offensive. "You're such a retard" was the ultimate insult. Who would choose to continue a pregnancy, knowing that the baby would be retarded?

These are just words. Some people might ask what difference it makes whether we say a baby is retarded or cognitively delayed. It makes all the difference in the world, since one label implies a static and unredeemable essence, the other a malleable condition that can be shaped by society and environment. When it came to my own writing,

I thought long and hard about what it meant to use the term "freak" and whether it would be better to use some nicer, cleaner substitute. In the end, I went with "freak." It was partly out of deference to the way my subjects referred to themselves, since "freak" has been, at times, a badge of honor in the netherworld of carnival folk. But I did it also to preserve the grating ugliness of a world where people were singled out for the deviance of their bodies. To call someone a freak is to treat him as an object, undeserving of compassion and dignity. By contrast, a person with a disability is a human being entitled to the same rights and respect as other persons.

This news clearly hadn't reached the authors of the parenting books we found at a Barnes and Noble on the Upper West Side. "Although universally dreaded, Down syndrome is quite rare," read one book called *Pregnancy and Birth*. Another explained, "The baby is born with small features, a tongue that tends to stick out, and slanting eyes with folds of skin at their inner corners. The head is flat at the back, and the ears are unusual. The baby may be floppy, with hands and feet that are short and wide and have a single transverse crease across the palms and soles. He may also have a congenital heart disease." This description was so grotesque and clinical. As if the baby could be reduced to a set of predictable features that had nothing to do with his parents' genetic information. It continued, "Down syndrome sufferers usually have learning difficulties, although the degree of difficulty varies, and many Down syndrome children are near normal." I was dismayed to see people with Down syndrome referred to as "suffering" or "afflicted," to see that Down syndrome was lumped together with genetic diseases that cause intense pain or fatality, to find it frequently described only by a list of physical characteristics and the risk of "mental retardation." Were my baby's appearance and personality really so predictable?

Wasn't there more to know about him than the effects of one chromosomal error?

"We have nothing more to offer you," the books seemed to say. "We're written for the parents of perfectly normal, perfectly healthy babies. We're sure you can find what you're looking for in the Special Needs section."

Once we threw out the pregnancy guides, it didn't take us long to get the facts. Otherwise known as Trisomy 21, Down syndrome is caused by a genetic accident that results in an extra twenty-first chromosome. It is relatively common, affecting one out of every seven hundred to eight hundred babies born in North America. It has no target demographics. Although older mothers are more likely to conceive children with Down syndrome, it can happen to anyone, regardless of age, race, culture, or nation. Given its prevalence, research tends to be woefully underfunded. This is in part because Down syndrome is caused by a chromosome comprising more than three hundred genes, which means that it presents a staggeringly complex scientific puzzle. For reasons that nobody has yet been able to determine, its consequences vary widely from one person to another. Contrary to what the pregnancy books suggest, its impossible to predict on the basis of a genetic diagnosis what challenges will face a given individual, or what her particular abilities or temperament will be.

Beyond the basics, the information we found was dismaying. Most of the resources we consulted offered litanies of every medical, physical, and emotional stumbling block our child might face before he reached adulthood. He might have autism, cardiac disease, Hirschsprung's disease, celiac disease, seizures, hip dysplasia, respiratory infections, sleep apnea, strabismus, hearing loss, hyperthyroidism, atlantoaxial instability, leukemia, dry skin, dry hair, hyperextensible joints, tactile defensiveness, and flat feet. Other sources told us that he might be slower, gentler, more sociable, more prone to wandering, and more stubborn. He might teach us the lessons of patience, humility, and tolerance. Lots of books and websites told us that our son was an angel, or that God had chosen us to be his parents. I came away from all of this wondering where we would find Henry in the midst of this avalanche of symptoms and characteristics. How would we make room for our baby to develop an identity of his own, and would we be able to recognize it apart from his diagnosis?

At the point of despair, we remembered Michael Bérubé's remarkable book, *Life as We Know It*, about the first three years in the life of his son Jamie, who has Down syndrome. I had known Michael, who teaches American literature at Penn State University, for more than a decade. Our paths had crossed a number of times at conferences, and I once invited him to give a talk at Columbia. By sheer coincidence, *Life as We Know It* was the first book I ever reviewed, back when I was a graduate student who never imagined having children of my own. My interest in disability studies was purely academic, and I thought Michael Bérubé got it better than just about anyone else. Jon found Michael's book on our shelf and reread it while lying awake the night after Henry was born. The next day he brought it to me in the hospital, where its story took on an entirely new meaning now that I, too, found myself the parent of a baby with Down syndrome.

As soon as I got back on email, I sent a message to Michael telling him about Henry:

Dear Michael,
My husband Jon and I have been rereading your beautiful book, which suddenly has a new meaning for us. Last Monday morning our

second son Henry was born. Twenty minutes later we were told he had "features consistent with Down syndrome." And over the next few days this careful phrasing evolved into a more definitive diagnosis, although we still haven't received genetic confirmation. I think you can understand the shock of such news and the effort to manage the jarring disjunction between the particularity of your own beautiful baby and the category that others are already using to define him. In contrast to many of the books and articles we've already read, we've found your stories about life with Jamie to be so heartening and your perspective on what it means to have a disabled child so thoughtful and sensitive. I hope that we can find the kind of wonder and inspiration in Henry's arrival into our family that you have found in Jamie, and that he will teach us to see the world in new ways, as Jamie clearly has done for you. At any rate, you have been in my thoughts so much in the last days that I wanted to write and share our news with you.

very sincerely yours,

Rachel

I will always treasure the message he sent in response.

Dear Rachel,

Wow. My goodness. Well, let's just say I wasn't expecting this email. But first things first—a hearty welcome to Henry! May he always find the world as warm as his parents' arms. And congratulations to his wonderful parents! Of course, I know the parental shock well, though back in 1991 my information was so outdated that I thought Jamie's life expectancy would be about 21 or so—and now, of course, I couldn't bear the thought of having him with us for only five more years.

You're probably inundated with books and articles and advice, and worries about what the next couple of years—or next couple of decades—will bring. I don't want to wish away those worries; they're real worries, as you know, and the most immediate thing is Henry's health. I hope he's thriving and happy—and that all your doctors and medical personnel understand the concept of "healthy baby with Down syndrome." But over the next few months or so, you'll probably find that the truism is true: babies with Down syndrome are *babies first*. Henry may reach those grasping-crawling-talking-walking developmental milestones at his own pace, but he'll surely take the same delight in music and play and stimulation that his older brother does, and he'll surely be every bit as beautiful as he is now.

Most of all, I share your hope that you find in Henry's arrival the kind of joy we've experienced with Jamie. About our chaotic human lives one can make no promises, but here's the latest from him: just last month, Jamie proposed that he and I go to New York, because (as he pointed out) we haven't visited the city all year. And because he's now 16, I decided to stretch him a little. We dined Friday night at the Plataforma Churrascaria on 49th, played games at ESPN Zone til midnight, slept til 9, got up, hit the Metropolitan Museum at 11 on Saturday (he's on an early modern–baroque binge, and bought a coffee-table book of Caravaggio's greatest hits), went to the *Lion King*, grabbed a pastrami sandwich for dinner and a 2 train to BAM for some surrealist Japanese dance. Sunday morning it was salsa at Carnegie Hall. He was kinda bored from time to time at the surrealist dance, but then, plenty of other people were too. (Unlike the people who got up and left, Jamie just flipped through his Caravaggio book during the dead spots.) His only disappointment that evening was that we didn't take the Q train over the Manhattan Bridge. The rest of the weekend he spent rubbing his hands together in glee. I know this may seem a bit impertinent when you're dealing with a newborn, but Rachel, when Jamie was a little neonate, nothing made me feel more reassured than the testimonies of older parents with older children, who could tell me from experience that life—in its somewhat altered form—would indeed go on. So I hope this helps. What I'm saying is that you never know. The next few years might be a strain at times, but you're in the greatest city in the world at the best time in history for children with Down syndrome. I know you're inundated with advice, but entre nous, I'd say start the salsa concerts early.

Seriously, our hearts and thoughts are with you and Jon. We know very well how weird and disorienting this time can be. (May I forward your letter to Janet?) If you need to get in touch with us for any reason, please feel free to call.

And best wishes to all your family from all of ours,
Michael

What Michael understood better than any book was the importance—and difficulty—of separating our baby from his diagnosis. What the story he told about Jamie said to us was: your life is not over. You will be happy again. Like other children, your child will bring you joy and happiness and frustration. And he has the same potential for happiness as any other child. I've gone back to his note often in the years since Henry was born. I remember my despair, and how moved I was by Michael's encouragement and understanding. Every time I read it, I hope that one day I'll write something so meaningful to another parent at a time of such grief and disappointment.

BACK IN THE NICU, HENRY was struggling with some of the most common problems faced by newborns with Down syndrome. Instead of drawing in tightly to his midline, his arms and legs flopped outward like a frog. This was a classic sign of hypotonia, or low muscle tone. His weakness made feeding difficult. He had trouble sucking from a bottle, and the effort made him so tired that he would collapse with exhaustion. The rest of his milk had to be poured into a feeding tube, which ran from his nose into his stomach. The doctors were unsure whether the weakness was caused by his low muscle tone or two holes in his heart discovered during his first echocardiogram. About half of all babies with Down syndrome are born with heart defects which, until relatively recently, were often fatal. In the past, one reason to dread a diagnosis of Down syndrome was that it could lead to a short and painful life. Advances in pediatric medicine have made it possible to cure many cardiac problems, more than doubling the life expectancy of people with Down syndrome. According to our cardiologist, the openings in Henry's heart might close by themselves or gradually worsen until they required surgery. Only time would tell.

When I looked at my baby through the plastic wall of the incubator, it was hard to believe that there was anything wrong with him. He was pink and chubby, with tufts of dark hair sticking out from his head. His legs kicked busily, one foot perpetually escaping from the hospital blanket. If I stuck my hand inside his bubble, he grasped my finger. With his long pointy newborn nails and scaly feet, I thought he looked like a baby elf.

Compared with his neighbors in the NICU, Henry was a picture of health. They were both dark red and no bigger than my hand. They lay in their heated compartments without moving, their toothpick limbs bristling with wires and tubes. For much of the day they were bathed in eerie blue light to counteract jaundice. One of them was covered in fur.

Most babies in the NICU suffer from low birth weight, which is often associated with prematurity. Once a symptom of maternal poverty, low birth weight is on the rise among upper-middle-class women, thanks to the multiple births that can result from in vitro fertilization (IVF). The increased use of IVF has made the NICU a place where the disadvantaged and the privileged meet. Not yet marked by class or social background, these babies were all equally vulnerable, kept alive by machinery that beeped and hissed and hummed day and night.

If they had been born just a few decades ago, none of the babies in the NICU would have lived. In past generations, babies like this sometimes became "pickled punks," the carnies' term for fetuses preserved in jars of formaldehyde to be displayed along with the side-show's living attractions. They were so tiny, I thought it remarkable that any of them would survive. Two days after Henry arrived, I came into the NICU to find a bustle of activity surrounding the baby to his left. A yellow curtain was drawn around the crib, and I could hear a doctor barking orders at his staff. The next morning, Henry had a new neighbor.

Scenes like this only reinforced my sense of the NICU as a place of bizarre contradiction. With its bright lights, phalanxes of machines, and neatly stacked equipment, it projected an aura of confidence in the certainty of medical knowledge and expertise. The tiny babies struggling to survive suggested otherwise. The floor that housed the NICU was decorated in a way that sought to distract visitors from its grim realities. The walls were painted with colorful scenes from children's books like *The Very Hungry Caterpillar* and *Goodnight Moon*, and the ceilings of the elevators were decorated with stars and moons. I knew why they were there. I had seen gravely ill children peering up at them as they were transferred by gurney from one floor to another.

Posted around the halls were fliers announcing support groups for their families, and I felt grateful that our stay was unlikely to be long enough for us to join.

One day I was sitting with Henry when the hospital's pediatric geneticist came in, followed by a group of medical residents. They clustered around the incubator, as he pointed at my son. "This is a three-day-old baby boy with features suggestive of Down Syndrome," he told them. "Note the wide-set eyes, the open mouth, the shallow bridge of the nose." He reached into the incubator to demonstrate the floppiness of Henry's limbs by lifting them and letting them drop. He pointed out that the last segment of each pinkie finger was slightly crooked. The residents peered at my baby and nodded. Nobody spoke to me, and they moved on.

Other doctors were patient and attentive, drawing us diagrams of heart muscles and kidneys and carefully explaining their concerns. Everything was highly tentative. Nobody seemed to know whether there was anything wrong with our baby. We talked a lot about the potential medical causes for his weakness, what treatments might be required, and the care he might need after leaving the hospital. Our conversations were always about symptoms. Nobody spoke to us about Down syndrome and what it meant for his future or ours. Nobody asked what we were feeling or how we were coping with the unanticipated prospect of raising a child with a disability. Nobody offered to direct us toward people who had shared our experiences. When I asked the hospital's social worker whether there was a support group I could contact, she seemed at a loss. It was as if Henry were the only baby with Down syndrome ever to be born on her watch.

On the day I was supposed to leave the hospital my obstetrician, Dr. Lewis, finally appeared. I was dressed in the same clothes I had worn to the hospital forty-eight hours before. Thinking how much had changed since I last put on those shapeless black maternity pants, I collapsed into tears. She found me sobbing on the bed. My tears were infectious and she began to cry too. "I went back through all of your records," she sniffed. "I wanted to make sure I didn't miss anything so I showed them to my colleagues and everyone agrees there was nothing. There was no sign.

"There's a girl on our street with Down syndrome," she continued. "She's okay. She runs around and plays with the other kids."

At that moment, I hated her intensely. Her demeanor had been robotic throughout both of my pregnancies. Her care was chipper and competent, without the slightest hint of a person beneath. If I asked her opinion about anything, she would carefully recite the pros and cons, never disclosing any views of her own. Through my tears, I was curious to see someone emerging. For the first time, she seemed human, giving me a glimpse of vulnerability, regret. I didn't like what I saw. I had been a model patient, going to every appointment, enduring scans, probes, and tests, as well as the everyday discomforts of pregnancy, without complaint. She had assured me that my fetus was healthy. Now I blamed her for the baby upstairs and I wasn't about to take her offer of comfort. But it also felt good to have a target for my rage and disappointment.

"How is the baby?" she asked.

I told her about his weakness, the feeding problems, the hole in his heart.

Now she was on familiar terrain. She launched into the same description of the heart that we had already heard from the cardiologist. Her voice was mechanical, as if she had said those words many times before. Jon arrived to help me get home, and the curtain that had lifted to disclose a different view of Dr. Lewis closed permanently.

Christmas

THAT NIGHT WE MADE A feeble effort at recapturing the Christmas we had missed two days before. Jon and I had both grown up celebrating Christmas, although my family is Jewish. My father, whose atheism was formed in outspoken rebellion against his Orthodox grandparents, enjoyed the rituals of the tree, plum pudding, and crackling fire. Our house, which was so often dark and lonely, would fill with friends. Christmas was equally important to Jon's family, where it included mountains of presents and a late-night visit to church.

When Jon's parents heard the news about Henry, they dropped their own holiday plans and flew to New York on Christmas Day. I had mixed feelings about their arrival. I knew we could use their help. While they watched Noah, Jon could spend time with me at the hospital. But I was also worried. For years, Jon's parents and I moved politely around one another, nobody quite sure how to enter the other's orbit or whether we even wanted to try. Before meeting Jon, I had never known people like Bill and HuEllen, who often seemed to me like they had walked straight out of a short story by Flannery

O'Connor. I knew that my world was as alien to them as theirs was to me, and we had never managed to find much neutral meeting ground.

This time, I found their presence surprisingly comforting. HuEllen arrived wearing a velour sweat suit and Christmas socks, her frosted hair a bit out of place and her suitcase bursting with presents for Noah. Bill followed slowly behind, dragging more suitcases and bags. HuEllen filled the air with cheery observations about the weather and the people back home in Georgia. When she fell silent, Bill, who was a vet, would chime in cautiously with questions about Henry's health and treatment. I could tell he was worried, and talking about medical matters returned him to familiar territory. We had been strangers for so many years, but we were drawn together by our shared concern for a baby none of us had expected.

Before Bill and HuEllen arrived, I told Jon I couldn't bear it if they talked about God. Or even worse, if they acted like our baby was a tragedy. He told me he didn't think they would. As soon as we all got to the NICU, I knew he was right. After asking the nurse's permission to hold Henry, HuEllen reached through the tangle of tubes and wires, and carefully lifted him out of the incubator. She held him while he slept, stroking his hair and cheeks in a way that told me she thought he was as beautiful and precious as her three other grandchildren. I had always been unnerved by the way Jon's family seemed not to care about things like intellect and ambition, qualities my own background and life experience had taught me to value above all else. When I was growing up, I believed my father's approval was contingent on my academic success. At some point long ago I had internalized the equation of my value as a person with my professional accomplishments. Looking at HuEllen, I realized that if Henry wasn't the smartest kid in the class, if he didn't grow up to get a Ph.D. or head a multinational corporation, she would love him all the more.

Christmas

When I got home from the hospital the day after Christmas, celebration was the last thing on my mind. But HuEllen couldn't bear the thought of Noah missing the holiday. Although I was exhausted and sore, I made myself wrap Noah's Christmas presents and I watched while he ripped open the packages. It seemed so strange to be sitting in my living room surrounded by familiar people when so much had changed. Without our baby there, I could almost imagine that life could go back to the way it had been.

I dragged myself through Noah's bedtime routine, determined to make things as normal as possible for him, knowing that all too soon his life would be turned on its head.

Jon and I lay on our bed together before I fell asleep. We held hands and promised each other that we would get through this. I remembered a powerful moment in Michael's book where Janet says to him, "We can handle this." Thinking about her strength gave me a new sense of resolve. "This is not going to be a tragedy," I told Jon firmly. I had grown up in a house filled with sadness. My earliest memories are of my mother's illness: uncontrollable fits of coughing, a hospital bed in the living room, an experimental treatment that left her back studded with oozing sores. I remember feeling ashamed that she couldn't come to the parent-teacher conference at school. When one of my classmates asked where she was, I told him that she was sick. "What does she have," he asked, "the flu?"

Once I found a snail shell on our front porch. I brought it in to show my mother, who was lying in bed. I desperately wanted to crush it. Although she asked me not to, I insisted, pounding it with a spoon until it cracked open. To my horror, there was a snail inside. Once I had smashed the shell, the entrails were exposed, black and wriggling. She scolded me as I screamed in surprise and fear at the destruction I had caused.

One afternoon I came home, and she was gone. An ambulance had taken her away to the hospital, I was told. Some days later, the baby-sitter picked my sister and me up from school and took us to the book-store. I arrived home to find my father and her two best friends stretched out on the bed sobbing wildly. "Your mother is dead! Your mother is dead!" they screamed, pounding the mattress and tearing at their hair. I cried because the grownups were crying, but I was also thinking about my new book, which showed how to make hundreds of drawings, step by step. I passed the nights of Shiva with that book, burying my nose in the pictures if anyone asked me how I was feeling.

In the years that followed, someone always seemed to be crying.

"I won't let my children grow up in a house of sadness," I said to Jon.

He squeezed my hand tightly and nodded in agreement.

THE NEXT MORNING, I HEARD Noah calling from his crib. I wasn't sure I would be able to pick him up, but I wanted to be the first person he saw. I wanted him to know that, although I had disappeared for two days, I hadn't abandoned him. I was home and ready to take care of him.

As soon as I opened the door to his room he started to scream.

"Hi sweetie!" I said in my cheeriest voice.

His screams grew louder. "No mommy! No! No! No! Mommy go away!"

"But sweetie, it's me! I'm home," I said desperately, running over to hug him.

He hurled himself into a corner of his crib as far away from me as he could get, crying louder and louder.

I began to cry too, collapsing on the floor in deep, wrenching sobs.

Christmas

And that was how Jon found us, each alone and wild with sadness. I knew tears weren't the right response. I knew the solution wasn't to let Jon step in and make everything okay. But I couldn't help myself. I couldn't bear the thought of losing Noah, my whole, perfect child. A baby who had been so stunningly beautiful that people stopped on the street to stare at him. The one whom I loved so deeply I yearned to have another so I would know what his brother or sister would be like.

The Feeding Tube

WHEN HENRY WAS FIVE DAYS OLD, we were told that he was ready to go home. The doctors felt that his heart condition required no immediate treatment. Aside from weakness, he had no other medical complications.

"If he turns blue," our nurse from the NICU told us, not very reassuringly, "take him to the emergency room right away."

Since he could still manage to drink only a few milligrams of formula at a time, Henry would have to come home with his feeding tube. To our dismay, Jon and I were told we would need to learn how to insert and remove it ourselves. Nobody knew how long Henry would need the tube, and it had to be replaced every few days. The day before Henry was scheduled to leave the hospital, Jon and I met our nurse in the NICU for a lesson. She showed us how to measure a piece of tubing that could stretch from his ear to his stomach and cut it to size. Then she trimmed a broad, flat sheet of tape to fit the space between his ear and his nose. This would protect his skin from a second piece of tape—this one impossibly thin and sticky—that would affix the tube to his face. When all the pieces were ready, we had to quickly thread the tube into one nostril, through the hole in the back of his nasal cavity, down his throat, into his stomach. Once it was in place, we were to attach a syringe to its loose end and pump it gently while listening to his abdomen with a stethoscope. If we heard a puff of air, we would know it was in the right place and feeding could begin.

The nurse made all of this look easy, completing the whole process within less than a minute. "Now you try it," she said, handing me the tape and a roll of tubing. I hesitated before deciding that Jon should go first. As a child, Jon spent a lot of time helping out in the family veterinary clinic. His experiences made him less squeamish about the body than most people, but they weren't much good in the NICU. Getting the tube to go down the back of Henry's nose wasn't as simple as it looked. The tube wanted to point straight back, but it had to be guided firmly downward. Jon poked around in Henry's nose again and again, trying to find an opening.

We were told that none of this was painful, but Henry's reaction indicated otherwise. He turned a deep red, screwed up his face, and mewed hoarsely. His mouth opened and closed with rage. The more he squirmed, the harder it was to guide the tube into the appropriate passage. It was also difficult to know when the tube had reached its destination. Was it too short, resting uselessly somewhere in his esophagus? Was it too long, poking some organ beneath his tiny stomach? The only way to tell was by listening for the puff of air coming from the syringe. And this seemed like a job meant for an octopus. One hand had to elevate the syringe above the feeding tube, which was attached to a pole at the side of Henry's crib, while using a few fingers to give it a delicate pump. The other had to keep the stethoscope in place on the wriggling baby's stomach. It would have been useful to have at least two more hands to hold Henry down while all of this was happening.

The Feeding Tube

42

"Don't worry," the nurse said as she watched us practicing nervously. "I've never seen anyone put a tube into the lungs by mistake." It hadn't even occurred to us that the tube could go into his lungs. Now we had something else to worry about. My heart sank.

The truth was, I didn't want to take Henry back to our apartment. I wished he could stay in the hospital where other people, professionals with confidence and training, would take care of him. I wished he could go anywhere other than our home, where I could still wake up and, for a few sleep-blurred seconds, forget that he existed.

THE TUBE WOULD BE THE bane of our existence for the first weeks of Henry's life. In his book, Michael Bérubé describes how he and his wife, Janet, became pros at changing Jamie's feeding tube. In their determination to wean him off it, they would have contests to see who could get him to drink the most milk from a bottle.

Jon and I never did become experts, and I lacked the good humor to turn our struggles into a friendly competition. The tape that lay neat and flat on Henry's cheek at the hospital quickly got dirty and puckered. The tube itself was constantly getting tangled around his hands and neck. The more active he became, the more likely he was to pull it out of his nose, meaning that we had to go through the whole dreadful process of inserting it all over again. And in our eagerness to pump him full of nutrients, we were constantly overfilling his feeding syringe. When this happened, the liquid would drain slowly down the tube until his stomach was full. At that point, it would start to leak back up the tube, leaving him soaking in a pool of milk.

Before Henry was born, we had arranged to have a baby nurse come to live with us for the first two weeks of his life. Rosalyn had been recommended to us by a friend who had used her several years before. She had no formal medical training, although she had been a nurse's aide in Trinidad. I assigned Jon the task of calling her to find out whether she was prepared to deal with a baby like ours.

After hanging up the phone, he came to me in tears.

"What did she say?" I asked, expecting the worst. I was sure she had canceled, unwilling to work with our imperfect baby. "Did she change her mind about coming?"

He shook his head. "She said, 'What good news. I love babies with Down syndrome. They're so gentle and easy to take care of.'"

I cried too. It was the first time anyone had suggested that there was something good about the birth of our baby.

ROSALYN ARRIVED ON NEW YEAR'S DAY, thirty-six hours after Henry came home from the hospital. I heard the sound of the doorbell with a combination of relief and concern. We were exhausted and I welcomed the extra help. How wonderful to have someone else who could get up in the night to struggle with the bottle and the feeding tube and the dirty diapers. But Jon's parents had just left the day before. I hated the idea of having a stranger in our apartment when we were already dealing with so much that was strange and unexpected.

As soon as she walked in the door, Rosalyn took Henry in her arms. "What a big, beautiful boy you are," she crooned.

I looked at her skeptically. Everyone at the hospital had treated Henry as if he were incredibly weak and fragile.

"What's this?" Rosalyn examined the feeding tube, sucking her teeth with disapproval. "In Trinidad, we would never put a tube into such a strong, healthy baby."

I felt nervous. I wondered if she would try to undermine the doctors' instructions. Were we going to clash over Henry's care? What if her ideas were different from mine? How would I be sure he was getting what he needed?

The Feeding Tube

I soon discovered that there was no need to worry. Rosalyn was the gentlest, most unobtrusive person I had ever met. Living with her was almost like being alone in our apartment, but without the burden of caring for a medically fragile newborn baby. She brought nothing with her except a small bag, which sat in an out-of-the-way corner behind the couch. We were prepared to set up a mattress for her in the living room, but she insisted that she didn't need anywhere special to sleep. Remarkably, this seemed to be true. No matter when I got up in the night, I would find her sitting on the couch, holding Henry or watching him sleep in his bassinet. She brought a small radio with her and would pass the time by listening to talk shows with the sound turned down to an almost inaudible level. Occasionally during the weeks she stayed with us, I would find her dozing. She would rouse herself the moment Henry stirred or made the slightest noise. Through the haze of my own exhaustion, it didn't seem possible that anyone could survive on so little sleep. And she hardly ate anything. Whenever I went to the market, I asked what I could buy for her. Usually she said she didn't need anything, although once in a while she would let me bring her some yogurt, which she ate along with a slice of "Caribbean bread" she had stored in her bag. At dinner, she took a minuscule portion of whatever we were eating, always insisting that she wasn't hungry.

Mostly Rosalyn faded into the background, leaving us time to take care of Noah and see some friends. After a few days, Jon went back to work and I started to make the endless phone calls required to set up Henry's medical appointments and get him evaluated for early intervention services. Rosalyn had an intuitive sense of when to become invisible and when we might welcome her company. We discovered that once she got warmed up, Rosalyn was passionate about politics. In the month after Henry was born, the Democratic primaries for the

The Feeding Tube

45

2008 presidential election were in full swing. After putting Noah to bed, we would eat dinner while watching the debates and the results of the earliest primary elections. Rosalyn had many opinions, although she was never outspoken about her preferences. As we watched the debates, she would comment quietly on the candidates' performances. She seemed to lean slightly in favor of John Edwards, and she was decidedly skeptical about Barack Obama.

The one thing Rosalyn did have strong feelings about was the feeding tube. "In the hospital in Trinidad, we would feed a baby like Henry with a bottle, even if it took us an hour," she clucked. "A tube is for babies who are small small. Not for a big strong boy like this."

The first time the tube needed to be changed, we used the dining room table as a makeshift operating theater. We decided that Henry would lie on a changing pad surrounded by all of the necessary equipment. We brought a lamp in from the bedroom to give us extra light and pushed the chairs against the wall. Once we had everything set up, the procedure went very differently than it had in the hospital, where we had a nurse to guide us through our difficulties. Here, we were on our own. As Jon fumbled with the tubing, Henry wriggled furiously, his entire body turning an angry red color. His mouth opened and shut, and feeble, hoarse sounds came out. I stood nervously behind Jon, giving suggestions in a loud voice until he snapped at me and asked if I wanted to do it myself. "Fine," I said heatedly, knowing I was no more qualified to do this than he was. I don't remember which of us finally got the tube down Henry's throat. All I know is that it seemed to take us forever to get it in place. His nasal cavity seemed like it had been rearranged since the hospital, and it was impossible to tell whether we had actually managed to get the tube into his stomach. He moved his head from side to side as we struggled to stick the upper end to his cheek, wasting sheet after sheet of tape. Throughout the whole process, Rosalyn hovered in the background muttering softly under her breath. Although she didn't say much, we could feel her disapproval. When it was over, she swept Henry into her arms as if to save him from us. "You didn't like that at all, did you?" she said as she comforted him. "We're going to get rid of that nasty tube. We're going to drink all of our milk from a bottle."

Rosalyn was determined not to feed Henry through the tube. He was supposed to drink at least three ounces of milk every three hours, and she would sit patiently holding the bottle until he finished the last drop. This could take up to two and a half hours, leaving only half an hour of rest in between. He fell asleep repeatedly while feeding, and she woke him back up by gently tickling his feet or wiping him with a damp washcloth. She experimented with different positions, looking for the postures that kept him the most alert and willing to suck. Each morning, she would deliver a triumphant report on how many bottles Henry had managed during the night.

WHEN HENRY WAS TWO WEEKS OLD, I took him to see Gretta Claussen, an occupational therapist who had been described to me as a miracle worker. I couldn't imagine what she could do for a baby that was only two weeks old, but I felt the need to do something. When I called, she told me she wasn't accepting new clients but then gave us an appointment for the next day. Gretta sees patients in her large, serene apartment on the Upper West Side. She had a back room set up as a studio, with mats on the floor and equipment piled against the walls. There, she placed Henry on the floor, rolling him carefully from side to side. She showed me how to flex his limbs in toward the midline and guide his hands toward his mouth.

The Feeding Tube

"Watch for gestures and signs that he's trying to communicate with you," she told me. "These may be subtle at first, but it's important that you respond to them." I remembered the first time I understood that Noah had something to say. We were riding in a taxi. He was making loud, plaintive sounds and I worried that they might become cries at any moment. Suddenly, I realized he wasn't complaining. He was simply vocalizing, delighted by his newly discovered capacity to make sound. I found that if I puckered my mouth into an O, after a second or two he would copy me, while cooing energetically. I was talking to him and he was talking back! With all of my worry about Henry's health, it hadn't occurred to me to think he might do the same.

Gretta asked me about the feeding tube, which kept getting in the way as she moved him around. I told her that the doctors had prescribed it while Henry was in the hospital, but he hadn't used it since the first day we got home. We had a remarkable baby nurse named Rosalyn who was determined to get Henry to drink his milk, even if it took him three hours to finish a bottle.

"Then why do you still have the tube?" she asked gently.

I thought for a minute. "I'm not really sure. I guess it's because the doctors told us it should be there."

She nodded. "With a child like Henry, you'll find yourself surrounded by doctors who think they know what he needs. Sometimes you'll disagree. You know him best and you'll have to be his biggest advocate. It's going to be important for you to make your own decisions about what's right for him."

I thought about what Gretta was saying. I'm someone who likes to follow directions. They give me a sense of purpose and order. Never in my life have I disregarded the instructions of a doctor, or any other professional authority. But there's a first time for everything. I went home and I took out the tube.

The Feeding Tube

Dr. Zimmerman didn't approve of my decision. "It's a lot more important for him to gain weight than to take all of his nutrients through a bottle. He may burn more calories trying to feed than he's able to consume," he warned. "And then we'll need to reinsert the tube." Rosalyn demurred. Feeding tubes were for the convenience of doctors and nurses who weren't willing to take the time with the bottle. And so she sat up with our baby night after night, coaxing him to drink. Before Henry was born, we had decided we could afford to pay her for ten days. But when the ten days were up, we gave her the weekend off and begged her to stay for another week. And when that week was over, we begged for another. What she was doing for Henry was priceless. We could see him growing stronger and more coordinated by the day. We knew how important it was for him to learn how to feed, but we weren't sure we had the perseverance to do it ourselves. Even now, when I watch Henry suck down a glass of milk, I think of Rosalyn, who believed he could do it when nobody else did, and how right she was.

The Nursing Circle

AFTER FOUR WEEKS, WE HAD to let Rosalyn go home. Precious as she was, we knew we couldn't have her stay with us forever. While she was there, we could entertain a certain fantasy that our lives were unchanged. We could sleep through the night, knowing she would feed Henry, and we could treat Noah as if he were still our only child. But we couldn't afford more Rosalyn. And besides, it was time to make a place for Henry in our family.

The doctors at the hospital had been so concerned about Henry's weakness that they had discouraged me from breast-feeding. "You have other things to worry about," one doctor told me. "The bottle lets you know exactly how much milk is getting into him. And besides, breast-feeding is much more tiring. We don't want him to be exhausted."

So I had been dutifully pumping milk every two or three hours since the day Henry was born. But I was determined to try nursing. Things had gone badly with Noah, and I had given up after twelve weeks when he so clearly preferred a bottle to me. The bigger he got the more he resisted the breast, until the only way I could get him to nurse was while bouncing violently on an exercise ball, which somehow seemed to relax him. One morning I found myself bouncing, nursing bra open, bands of pain shooting up my back, while Noah cried in protest. I started to cry too, as I imagined what we must look like. Then I had to laugh. I realized it was time to stop the whole ridiculous routine. From then on, Noah took all of his milk from a bottle and never looked back. After it was too late, I wished I had tried harder to make the nursing work. I thought that early separation must have shaped our relationship. Noah didn't like to be held very much and had a strong need to be independent of me. He was an irritable baby who always wanted to be in motion and liked to be held in a standing position long before he could support himself on his own legs. His temperament changed completely on the day he turned one, which was also the day he took his first steps. Once he could move himself around he became a different person, in love with the ability to explore the world on his own terms.

I couldn't let this happen with Henry. He needed me too much, and I needed him. While Rosalyn was still with us, I had two appointments with a lactation consultant. She was optimistic about Henry's strength and muscle tone, insisting that the effort required to nurse would be good for the weakness in his mouth and cheeks. She gave us a lot of tips about positioning and told us to keep trying. But it was so easy to let Rosalyn take care of Henry's feedings, and I had so much else to do, that I hadn't been trying very hard. Once Rosalyn was gone, we began practicing a lot, and—quite miraculously—my baby, who had been so weak and fragile he could hardly suck from a bottle, became a good eater. He wasn't at all confused about moving back and forth from breast to bottle, seeming to like both equally well. And best of all, nursing made me feel close to him in a way that I had never felt with Noah when he was a baby.

Still, I worried constantly about whether Henry was getting proper nourishment. Because of his muscle weakness, it was all the more important that he have enough milk to keep his strength up.

Instead of having the lactation consultant come back for a third time, I decided to go to a breast-feeding support group. I knew there would be a scale to weigh Henry before and after the feeding, which would tell me exactly how much milk he had consumed. It seemed like a good way to get out of the house, and I liked the idea of doing something ordinary, like any other mother and baby.

The meeting began with a chance to weigh our babies. Then we sat in a circle, opened up our shirts, and fed our babies en masse. While we did so, the consultant asked us to go around the room and tell her what concerns had brought us to the group. Any woman who has had a baby knows that, aside from sleep, feeding is the paramount anxiety in the first three months of life, when otherwise intelligent people find themselves intently scanning dirty diapers for the quality and quantity of their contents, talking endlessly about burping, spitting up, latching on, foremilk and hindmilk, reflux and projectile vomiting. All the while, your body is exhausted and raging with unfamiliar hormones. Among new mothers, feeding is a deeply emotional issue. More than one woman cried as we went around the circle, her oversized nipples bared for all the group to see. There was a woman with one "gusher" that spewed milk into her baby's mouth with such velocity that he gagged and refused to continue. Another's baby was losing weight because she didn't have enough milk, despite dosing herself on herbs, vitamins, and a special diet. One woman had nipples that were too big for her baby's mouth, another's nipples were too inverted for sucking, and yet another's were cracked and bleeding from improper latch. Some babies woke up too often in the night, others slept for too long. Someone wanted advice about how to wean

The Nursing Circle

her baby off the breast, and someone else wanted to know how to encourage her baby to prefer breast to bottle.

I listened to all of this with a mounting sense of dread. As my turn approached, I started to feel that it was a terrible mistake to be there. The problems I was hearing about seemed so pedestrian. I had been through this before. Within a few months, I knew that these troubles would resolve themselves. The other babies in the room would start to eat solid food and sleep through the night. Then they would walk and talk. Then one day they would go to kindergarten, and then to college. I felt close to tears. When it came time to share my story, I would stop the room cold. Why had I come? Would I be asked to leave? These women thought they had problems, but what did they know? I would show them problems.

It was my turn.

I took a deep breath. "This is Henry. He's five weeks old and he has Down syndrome." The words felt unfamiliar on my tongue. "I want to breast-feed. But he may have heart disease, and he was born with low muscle tone, so it's especially important that he get enough milk."

The consultant looked concerned, but not unduly so. "You do need to be careful. Are you giving him bottles to supplement?"

I nodded. "I'm so confused about what's getting into him. I just want to know whether the breast-feeding is working at all."

"Before we go any further, let's weigh him and see how much milk he's taken in."

I took him over to the scale, feeling the eyes of the group at my back, imagining their pity and their gratitude that they weren't standing in my shoes.

After I put Henry on the scale, I had to look at the numbers twice. He was four ounces heavier. That meant he had consumed four ounces of milk. More than he had ever been able to drink out of a bottle. More weight than any other baby in the room had gained during the session. "Four ounces," I reported.

"That's wonderful!" the consultant crowed.

Four ounces. I looked around, realizing I was the only one who had no problem. My nipples were doing just fine, and so was my baby. In fact, my baby was the best eater in the room!

I walked out of the meeting elated. I would be able to nurse my baby. Henry had shown the doctors how wrong they were. I had also said the words "Down syndrome" out loud and the meeting hadn't come to a screeching halt. Nobody acted like I shouldn't be there. And nobody seemed to think my baby was a tragedy.

On the way home, we stopped at the corner for a red light. The woman next to me leaned over the stroller and cooed, "Isn't your baby perfect!"

A few hours before, I might have disagreed. But at that moment, I believed she was right and I nodded in agreement that, yes, in his own way, he was.

What Peggy Did

IN THE HOURS AFTER HENRY was born, the only way I could assimilate the bigger, more cataclysmic news about Down syndrome was by fixating on small things. Would his belly button be an "outie" once the stump of umbilical cord fell off? What if he had the sharp, pointy teeth I remembered from pictures of people with Down syndrome? How would we explain Down syndrome to Angela, our Dominican nanny? Worst of all, I was tormented by the thought that Henry wouldn't be able to go to daycare with Noah.

In September, Noah had started attending Basic Trust, a warm, unassuming daycare center housed in the basement of a church on West 99th Street. Long before he was accepted there, we realized that "BT"—as insiders call it—inspires a cultlike devotion among parents and alumni, many of whom graduate from college swearing it was the most meaningful educational experience of their lives. Much of this had to do with its director, Peggy Sradnick, a small, fierce person with a raunchy sense of humor, a warm heart, and strong opinions about everything. Often her opinions were solicited, since she seemed to know everything there was to know about raising children from birth to kindergarten. But sometimes she dispensed them without invitation or the slightest effort at self-censorship, like the disapproving lecture she gave about my birth plan when I was eight months pregnant. Peggy had accused another mother of causing her son's biting problem, and she told someone else that her beloved nanny was the reason why her child wasn't toilet trained. I survived Peggy by listening when I thought she had something important to say and tuning out the occasional bombast.

We weren't particularly interested in the cult of BT when we went looking for daycare. We simply wanted to find a place where Noah would be happy and well cared for: getting into daycare in Manhattan can be harder than getting into college. We were turned away by every other center in our neighborhood, but Noah was admitted to BT largely because I work with Eileen, who was Peggy's best friend. It was expensive, but he could stay there all day, with lunch and snacks included. Another parent who had done the math insisted that—by the hour—BT was the best deal around, since so many of the other centers in the neighborhood closed for long stretches on holidays and over summer vacation. Once Noah started in the fall, we quickly fell in love with his teachers, the ugly, sagging furniture and scuffed walls, and the feeling of being part of a community.

We soon discovered that Peggy was the essence of BT. We didn't send Noah there until he was one and a half, but some babies go to BT when they're only three months old. For their families, the experience of parenting is completely bound up with the experience of BT. Peggy was there when we arrived in the morning, chatting with parents and teachers, barking at children who were being too rough or too loud, or simply surveying the terrain from the elevated walkway that divided the Big Kids' Room from the gym. On parent nights, we sat in a circle while Peggy told us what our children had been up to and dispensed advice about how to manage them when they weren't at school. Fund-raisers invariably involved poker, Peggy's favorite game. The hottest item at the silent auction was a stack of T-shirts imprinted with the words "What would Peggy do?"

We didn't buy a T-shirt. We were less caught up in the cult of Peggy than many other parents. What we loved about BT was that it made Noah happy. For the first few days, he cried and begged me not to leave. But soon enough, he didn't want to go home in the afternoons. Noah made his first friends at BT. They would greet each other with rough hugs, falling to the floor with shrieks of delight. We were amazed to see him doing things that seemed far beyond his sixteen-month abilities, like drinking out of an open cup, sitting in a circle for meeting, and taking a nap in a room filled with other kids. For the first time, he had a life separate from us. He would come home singing songs we didn't know, wanting to play games someone else had taught him. When I asked about his day, he would shrug like a teenager, enjoying the fact that he belonged to a world that didn't include me.

Some of my friends' children went to daycare centers where the staff would report episodes of misbehavior and note skills and behaviors that needed improvement. The teachers at BT seemed to look only for the positive, finding what was unique and interesting about each child. They wrote us notes about the funny things Noah did during the day, turning his most trying habits into interesting quirks of personality. When he kept the entire center awake by singing the Dreidel Song at the top of his lungs, we got a note describing him as "the songbird of naptime." During the summer when he refused to let us dress him in shorts, we could bring them to BT knowing he would put them on for his teachers without a fuss. When he became obsessed with baseball, nobody minded that he wore an increasingly filthy Yankees jersey every day for months. The teachers even wrote "Jeter" in place of his name on the attendance board. We couldn't imagine a happier place for Noah to spend his time until he was ready to go to kindergarten.

AS I LAY IN THE HOSPITAL, I was consumed by fear that Henry would be shut out of the warm, magical world that had become so important to Noah and to us. I knew there were other, more pressing things to worry about. But the thought that he would be rejected by BT seemed like the greatest tragedy I could imagine.

As soon as BT reopened after the New Year, we made an appointment to see Peggy. We thought she could help us figure out what kinds of therapy Henry would need. We were also worried about Noah. It was hard enough to have a new baby brother, let alone one who needed so much extra care. We wanted her reassurance that his teachers would help him through this difficult time, as well as any advice she might have to offer about how to make things easier at home.

We had already told her the news about Down syndrome by email. I tried to tell people by email rather than in person became then I didn't have to exert so much energy managing their feelings. I had too much else to worry about.

"Okay guys, this is big," she said as we settled in her office after dropping Noah off. I felt affirmed. She recognized the enormity of our situation. She wanted to know everything. How had this happened? How had we learned the news? How was Henry's health?

We told her as best we could. When we were finished, she leaned forward.

"I want him," she said firmly. "I want him here at BT. He can come to BT whenever he's ready."

It was hard to believe what I was hearing. Without knowing the extent of Henry's disability, Peggy was saying that he could go to school like any other child. The rest of our meeting passed in a blur. Peggy leapt into action, rifling through a worn Rolodex for the names of therapists and parents she knew in the Special Needs world, scribbling information on a yellow Post-it and ordering me to start making calls as soon as I got home.

It wasn't until we got out into the hallway that I fully realized what had just happened. Our baby was wanted. When the time came, he would have a place alongside his brother, and with other children. He would spend his days in a place where people saw the best in him, focusing on what he was doing rather than telling us all of the things he wouldn't be able to do. This dingy corridor, with its annoying clutter of strollers, tricycles, and sand toys, would welcome Henry into BT, just as it had Noah.

WHEN HENRY GOT OLDER, Peggy allowed him to work with his physical therapist in the BT gym. She seemed surprised that, at fifteen months, he was still nowhere near walking. I told her I didn't expect him to be walking for at least another year.

She shook her head. "Of course he'll walk much sooner than that," she said vehemently.

I disagreed. By that time, I had learned to stop predicting when Henry would reach any developmental milestones. I was confident he would walk at some point, but I also knew that setting deadlines only led to frustration and worry. Nonetheless, I liked Peggy's sense of conviction. I liked that she believed Henry would walk sooner rather than later.

As it turned out, Peggy was wrong. Henry took his first steps a few weeks after his second birthday.

She didn't live to see it happen.

The way I learned about Peggy's illness was bizarre. One day in June, I got an email with the subject line "Peggy's Good News." When I opened it, I found this message:

Dear BT Community,
Yesterday, Peggy's surgery went about as well as it possibly could. Though there are still some tests to do, the neurosurgeon believes the growth in Peggy's cerebellum was benign and she is on her way to a full recovery. She will probably be out of intensive care today and moved to a regular room. As soon as we have more info about her willingness to see people or take calls, we'll let you know.

This didn't sound like "good news" to me. Nobody had told me anything about surgery. Or about a growth. I didn't even know Peggy was in the hospital. I later discovered that my address had been left off of the message announcing the operation. BT wasn't known for its office management, and apparently each computer had a different email list. I learned that Peggy had been experiencing nausea, dizziness, and headaches for a while. Her doctors had determined that the symptoms were caused by a brain tumor, which had to be surgically removed and tested for malignancy. The "good news" was that it was benign.

After the operation, Peggy began a long process of recovery. BT parents and friends kept us apprised of her condition on an upbeat blog called "oyveypeggy." One post included a picture of Peggy eating lobster in her hospital bed, and another showed her taking a nap with her daughter, who had flown in from Oregon. In July she was moved to a rehab center. Noah and I sent brownies and a drawing with a teacher who was planning to visit. We read that Peggy ate steak on her sixty-fourth birthday, took an afternoon off to go shoe shopping, and felt annoyed by physical therapy. We heard that she might be well enough to attend the BT graduation in early August.

Peggy wasn't at the graduation. Instead, we got an email saying that an infection had sent her back to intensive care. Her condition was critical. No visitors were allowed.

After graduation, BT closes for a long two-and-a-half-week stretch. That year, we rented a house in the Berkshires, which turned out to be a terrible idea. The house that had looked so charming in the vacation rental photos turned out to be small and run down. There was only one bathroom and it was at the top of a steep, narrow staircase that wasn't safe for either of the children. We had to pile furniture and suitcases at the bottom to stop Henry from trying to climb it. The weather was too hot, there were too many bugs, and everybody was in a bad mood. We wanted to go home but we had promised a friend she could come and stay with us at the end of the week.

On Tuesday, I opened my email to find that Peggy was dead. The infection had worsened; she slipped into a coma and never woke up.

I didn't have time to cry when I first read the message. Jon was in the shower and Noah was screaming at Henry for knocking his trains over. I've cried a lot since then. My tears were partly about losing Peggy, but also over the recognition that there have been too few women like her in my life. I don't often go searching for surrogate mothers; in fact I tend to run away from anyone who might fill that role. But when I let myself imagine what it would have been like to have a mother, she's a lot like Peggy: brash, loving, honest to the point where it hurts.

Peggy's family had planned a memorial for the next day. There was no way we could go, so I sent a message to be read during the service. I thanked Peggy for giving Noah a second home at BT. And

I wrote about how much it meant to us when she said she wanted Henry. "Peggy appreciated what each child has to offer. We have had to accept that there are places where Henry will not be welcome. We will remember her for making sure that BT would never be one of those places." I know many people enjoyed Peggy's impetuous generosity, but Henry gave her an opportunity to prove how genuinely she believed in her own principles. "We let the children into our lives," read the BT website, "and together we explore the world as part of a rambunctious family." Without reservations, she had made Henry a part of that family.

One day after BT reopened for the fall, Henry came with me to drop Noah off. I put him down on the floor to play while I helped Noah get settled. When I got ready to go, I realized he was nowhere to be found. I ran out into the hall, worried that he would fall down the stairs or get into the sand table. I found him in the Baby Room, sitting on a miniature couch with some other kids. A teacher was reading *Five Little Ducks*, which is one of his favorite books. He didn't notice me, and I stepped back out of view so that I could take a minute to watch him laughing and pointing along with the others.

PART TWO

Aiming High Enough

FROM THE TIME HE WAS about two weeks old, Henry loved to lie on his back with one arm sticking up, waving his hand in the air. He would stay like this for long stretches, studying his fat, stubby fingers as if they were the most interesting things in the world. I took this pose to be a gesture of self-regard, a curiosity about the possibilities and limits of his own body. But it was also an early sign of socialization. Henry was trying to extend himself into the world beyond his body and was making a gentle request to be acknowledged by others. Many months later, the first word he learned to sign would be "more," which he used to demand food, attention, and play. His speech therapist called this "generalizing," applying one word to every context for lack of a better substitute. True enough, but I also saw it as an outgrowth of the waving arm, an expansive welcome to the world and all it had to offer.

Since nearly everything that happened in the weeks and months after Henry was born made me cry, just thinking about the waving hand could bring me to tears. I imagined what might have happened to our baby if he had been born in a different time and place. Doctors would probably have suggested that we commit him to an institution for the feebleminded. I pictured him spending his days lying in a crib, his hand waving back and forth with nobody there to notice. His gesture unacknowledged, eventually he might have given up trying to communicate. The truth is that not so long ago, parents were routinely advised to institutionalize babies with Down syndrome, who were classified as "mongoloid idiots." Just as I had once collected the stories of freaks, I became preoccupied with collecting stories of Henry's predecessors. There's Dwight Core Jr., a boy with Down syndrome who was committed to an institution at the age of six. I learned about him from the film *Think of Me First as a Person*, a documentary made by his nephew, George Ingmire. Dwight appears to have been a happy, curious child. There are scenes of him playing with a garden hose, swinging in the backyard, and opening Christmas presents with his family. These images are a devastating contrast to footage of the institution where Dwight was housed, which show half-naked children crowded aimlessly together with no caregivers in evidence. Dwight's father, who shot the film, seems genuinely appalled by what he sees, but he is determined to do what the experts had advised was best for Dwight and his family, which is to institutionalize his young son.

There's also Judith Scott, who was institutionalized with Down syndrome at age seven after school authorities pronounced her ineducable. Nobody noticed that she wasn't following their instructions because she couldn't hear them. In fact, it would take another thirty-three years for anyone to realize that Scott was profoundly deaf. By that time she was living at the Gallipolis Developmental Center, where the staff decided she should learn American Sign Language (ASL)—a pointless recommendation since nobody who worked there knew how to sign. Scott would almost surely have died unremembered had she not been rescued by her twin sister, Joyce, in 1985. Over the next twenty years, Scott became an accomplished fiber artist whose work has been exhibited around the world.

Then there's Daniel Miller, who became known to the world in 2007, when an article in *Vanity Fair* magazine made the shocking revelation that the playwright Arthur Miller had a son with Down syndrome. Just a few days after Daniel was born to Miller and his third wife, Inge Morath, in 1966, he was placed in the facility where he lived until adulthood. By all accounts, Daniel survived his harrowing experience unscathed, becoming a successful, loving, and well-adjusted adult. Miller never acknowledged Daniel's existence, and some have speculated about how this painful secret influenced his work. Scott, Core, and Miller were victims of a society that believed people with Down syndrome were unable to learn anything beyond the most basic rudiments of self-care. The birth of such children was viewed as a tragedy. At a time when the problem of disability was typically resolved by attempting to hide it from view, parents of babies with intellectual disabilities were advised to forget they existed, to send them away and tell people they had died at birth.

Such views were still the norm in 1974, when Emily Perl Kingsley, one of the early writers for *Sesame Street*, gave birth to her son Jason. She remembers the doctors telling her: "Your child will be mentally retarded. He'll never sit or stand, walk or talk. He'll never be able to distinguish you from any other adults. He'll never read or write or have a single meaningful thought or idea. The common practice for these children is to place them in an institution immediately." Unlike Miller and Core, Kingsley defied the advice of medical authorities by taking Jason home and raising him alongside his siblings. When Jason was a teenager, she helped him to cowrite (along with his best friend Mitchell Levitz, who also has Down syndrome) the book *Count Us In*, about growing up with Down syndrome. She devoted her career to making people with Down syndrome visible by including them on *Sesame Street*. For the generations of kids who grew up watching the show, it's hard to understand how radical Kingsley's decision was. We've come to assume that on *Sesame Street* diversity includes an array of cognitive and physical abilities, as well as people of different genders, races, and ethnicities. But at a moment when people with disabilities were largely voiceless and invisible to the public eye, Kingsley realized how transformational it could be to feature them on TV doing the same things as everybody else.

After I finished *Count Us In*, I searched Columbia's library catalogue for old books on Down syndrome, trying to imagine what it must have been like to be a mother in the past. I discovered that Down syndrome took its name from the nineteenth-century doctor who first identified the condition. In many ways, John Langdon Down had a remarkably progressive view of intellectual disability. He gave up a lucrative career to establish Normansfield Institute in southwest London, where people with disabilities were supervised by staff who treated them with care and respect. Clients were exposed to song, dance, and theater, as well as workshops, vocational training, and outings in the community. Down was credited with the expression "aim high enough," which, some one hundred years later, would be adopted as the slogan for World Down Syndrome Day. "Aim high enough" was intended to commemorate Down's achievements with a rejoinder to those who still questioned the potential and abilities of people with Down syndrome. By taking on appropriate challenging goals, they would show just how much they could accomplish.

I also read about Down's more unsavory legacy. Obsessed with classification, he believed that "congenital idiots" (a category that included Down syndrome) could be grouped according to ethnic phenotype. Because of their allegedly Asiatic features, people with Down syndrome were classified as "mongoloid idiots." This view was radical in that it insisted on the humanity of people with intellectual disabilities. But it also mistakenly racialized them. As late as the 1920s people continued to hold the belief that the features of Down syndrome were a throwback to an earlier Mongolian ancestry. While these theories were eventually debunked, the tendency to see people with Down syndrome as primitive, childish, or unfinished persists even in the present.

Another unfortunate misunderstanding among earlier generations of specialists in Down syndrome was the belief that parents, and particularly mothers, were responsible for the children's disability. According to one textbook from the 1920s, "the sole and adequate cause of mongolian imbecility is to be sought in the condition of the mother during pregnancy." Another author wrote, "some abnormal condition in the mother during pregnancy was reported in more than twice as many of the mongolians as control mothers." A third text associated Down syndrome with a "psychosomatic disorder" in mothers who were "high strung, nervous, easily upset." The books are filled with photographs of chromosomes and cells. Charts and graphs tracking the mothers' ages and social and medical histories give their claims the authority of scientific research. How would it feel for the mother of a child with Down syndrome to read these books? And how would the doctors who read them treat the women who gave birth to such children?

There are also pictures of body parts: skulls and brains, ears, eyes, feet, and wide, stubby-fingered hands. One book includes pictures of people. There is no effort to conceal their identities, as is the convention in most modern medical textbooks. It's as if the author assumes that it doesn't matter, since the subjects are incapable of understanding enough to care whether they are exposed as clinical specimens. Boys and girls stared out at me from the pages. Regardless of gender, their hair is cropped carelessly close to the skull, jaws slack and eyes dull. Their postures are stooped or asymmetrical, and their limbs flop out to the sides. They are dressed in coarse, institutional clothing that makes them look more like prison inmates than children. One boy twists his hyperflexible legs into a pretzel shape. On facing pages I found photos of a girl and a woman who had clearly been asked to sit with their mouths open, a posture associated with idiocy. Each exposes a thick, lumpy tongue that hangs down past her chin. "The Mongol is always mentally deficient," wrote Dr. Kate Brousseau in 1928. "The majority of these children are in the imbecile group and only a few of them reach the mental age of 6 or 7 years. Many Mongols, however, belong to the idiot class having a mental age of less than two years." This doctor advised against keeping such children in the home. Parents were unable to provide adequate training, she opined, and the child's presence was "often harmful to other members of the family." Therefore, "it is advisable that he should be placed as early as possible in an institution where he may receive proper care and training." Because most of these children didn't live beyond the age of 14, she explained, there was little point in educating them. They "are practically unimprovable and can be taught to perform only the simplest tasks." I could see why a doctor in the 1920s would believe that children with Down syndrome couldn't be educated. Warehoused in institutions where they received little stimulation or personal attention, they simply had no motivation to develop.

We live in a different age. The doctors who saw Henry gave him their best care. Nobody suggested that his life would be short or that he was incapable of learning. Before we even left the hospital, we were put in contact with an agency that would coordinate our early

intervention services, which would provide us with a team of therapists, each trained to work on some aspect of his physical and cognitive development. Henry was lucky that his health was good enough
to allow him to start right away.

In the first weeks of Henry's life, I was haunted by the loss of the
child I imagined I would have and by fears about what the strange
baby who had taken his place would become, or fail to become. I
couldn't sleep much, and when I did, I'm not proud of the dreams I
had: nightly freak shows of squat, stubby-limbed creatures who
grunted and drooled their way through my mind. To drive them
away, I threw myself into the task of organizing Henry's medical
appointments and getting him the best possible team of therapists as
quickly as I could. The busier I was, the less time I had to think about
what had become of my plan to have the perfect family.

Early intervention starts with a series of evaluations by physical,
occupational, and feeding therapists, a special educator, and a social
worker. Our first evaluation was like something out of a slapstick
comedy. It was scheduled for a morning when Noah was home from
daycare. In the weeks since Henry's birth, Noah had decided he
wasn't happy about the presence of this strange new infant and his
companion, Rosalyn. From his two-year-old perspective, she must
have seemed as permanent as his baby brother. Noah hadn't taken his
unhappiness out on Henry, whom he hardly deigned to acknowledge.
Instead, he had rejected all other outsiders. It was as if, having already
allowed Rosalyn and Henry to invade our lives, he was determined
to prevent anyone else from coming in, even temporarily. His resistance took unpredictable forms, but it always involved behavior
disruptive enough to derail all social interaction. When friends came
over, he would throw himself into violent tantrums, make urgent and
constant demands for food and drink, or insist that we hide with him

in another room until the guests went away. After too many visits ended in disaster, we had temporarily stopped inviting people to our apartment.

I was worried about how Noah would respond to the evaluator. I knew I should have rescheduled the appointment as soon as I realized that he would be home. But I was in a hurry to get the assessments over with so that Henry's services could begin. When the therapist arrived, I opened the door with a sick feeling. No sooner had she come into the apartment than Noah began to whine and fuss for my full attention. His complaints quickly escalated into loud shrieks. As we sat down to go through a family questionnaire, Noah started to jump on the furniture, pulling at my hair and clothes. The therapist spread Henry on a blanket on the floor, as far from Noah's frenzied acrobatics as possible. It was hard to pay attention to what she was doing with a crazed toddler trying to climb my leg, and at first I didn't notice when she started to cough and rub her eyes.

"Do you have any pets?"

I shook my head.

"Did an animal ever live in this apartment?"

"Not that I know of."

"Because I'm severely allergic." She began to grope in her bag, spilling papers and therapy tools onto the floor. "I must have left my inhaler in the car." She was wheezing and seemed panicked.

Noah tugged at my arm, screaming, "MOMMY MOMMY MOMMY MOMMY! I want you to come play in my room! I want that lady to go!"

"I can't breathe," she gasped, her eyes red and streaming. "I think it's the rug. An animal must have been on the rug."

I had seen the rug delivered, brand new, still encased in a plastic sheath. I knew no animal had ever touched it, but this was no time for arguments. "Let's get you away from it," I suggested, attempting to guide her into the kitchen while carrying Noah, who was kicking and twisting wildly, heavy as a bag of cement. Stray Cheerios left over from breakfast crunched underfoot as I shoved him into the highchair and poured half a box of cookies onto the tray. I opened the window, and the therapist pressed her face to the screen, gasping as she inhaled the frigid January air.

"I want that lady to go! Go away, lady!" Noah cried.

After a few more breaths, she wiped her eyes and declared herself recovered enough to return to Henry, who was still lying placidly on his blanket in the living room. When I went back to check on her a few minutes later, she blew her nose, coughed wetly, and said she had everything she needed. It seemed like she had barely looked at Henry. I couldn't imagine that this was the most thorough evaluation she had ever completed. I walked her to the door, telling her how sorry I was, although I'm not sure what for—the air quality in my apartment? My dirty living room rug? That I had a baby who required her to be there at all?

I shut the door behind her and took a deep breath. I could hear Noah calling from the kitchen, where he was still a captive in his high chair. It was only 9:30 A.M.

The rest of the evaluators came together in a team. They crowded into our living room, bustling around while Henry lay calmly on his blanket. One woman waved a red plastic ring in front of his eyes, while another examined his grasp and the strength of his arms, legs, and trunk. A feeding specialist asked me to give Henry a bottle so that he could observe his suck-swallow coordination, listening intently to the loud wheezing noises he made as he struggled to breathe. In the middle of this, a social worker interviewed me about our family and friends, busily jotting down everything I said. And then, just as quickly as they had come, they were gone.

Aiming High Enough

My baby was just three weeks old. He looked healthy and content to me. I wondered what the therapists saw when they looked at him. How could you evaluate the mental health of a baby who was less than a month old? Or his speech? Did he already have physical and developmental delays? It all seemed pretty dubious, but absorbing myself with this process helped me to avoid the much harder questions about what the future would hold.

It took several weeks for the completed evaluations to arrive. I had been warned that the evaluators were likely to describe Henry's condition in the most negative terms. With a diagnosis of Down syndrome, he was certain to get services, but the more dire his prognosis, the easier it would be to get him what he needed. I knew this was coming. Still, when a big manila envelope arrived with the name of the evaluating agency printed on the outside, I hesitated to open it. Between us, Jon and I had nearly twenty-five years of higher education, three master's degrees, two Ph.D.s, and a J.D. We had gone far in life by being extremely good test takers. It was chastening to read the reports prepared by Henry's evaluators, who pronounced him far below average in gross motor, fine motor, cognition, and speech. Dumb as it may sound, the overachiever in me was gratified to see that I came across well to the social worker, who wrote, "Mother was able to provide adequate information regarding Henry's development, and appeared to have some awareness of developmental risks and delays. Mother seemed to be closely bonded with Henry, and was cooperative and easily engaged."

Armed with these reports, we prepared for our meeting with the early intervention official designee, otherwise known as the EIOD, the city official who would decide which services Henry would receive, and how often. We would be joined by Sarah Lee, the early intervention service coordinator assigned to help us navigate the system. Sarah ("just like the baker," she told me cheerfully at the beginning of our first phone conversation) was earnest and thorough, and I liked her immediately. It was hard for me to believe that her entire job was to support our efforts to get our baby the care he required.

Sarah warned us that these meetings were unpredictable, depending a great deal on the generosity of the EIOD assigned to our case. Sometimes parents got everything they requested without any trouble at all, and sometimes every last thing was a struggle. She would be there to advocate for us, but there was no way to know in advance which official would show up at our meeting.

We arrived prepared for battle. I had made copies of Henry's evaluations, his medical reports, and a long typed list of talking points about the services he should receive. Jon and I had rehearsed what we would say and the arguments we would offer if we met with any resistance. It turned out that none of this was necessary. Loretta, our EIOD, was kind and sympathetic, listening patiently as we marched through our prepared speech and then granting our every request. Whereas some EIODs take the stance of gatekeepers against families trying to work the system, Loretta believed it was her job to match children with the services they needed. She later told us that she has an adult daughter with a disability and could understand from her own experience what it was like to be on our side of the table. By the end of the meeting, we had determined that Henry would be assigned physical, occupational, and speech therapists, who would each come twice a week. Loretta even asked whether we wanted to add a special educator, who could visit us twice a month to help Henry with play and socialization. Although I couldn't imagine how a baby of less than two months old would work on socialization, I nodded enthusiastically.

And what about a social worker to help our family adjust to the demands of caring for a baby with disabilities? She could come once a week for an hour.

I nodded in agreement. I figured as long as we had someone generous in the room, it was best to take everything she offered. Maybe the next EIOD wouldn't be so cooperative. I couldn't quite believe how smoothly it had all gone. I sat nervously as Loretta started to fill out our paperwork, feeling like we were getting away with something.

She stopped writing and looked up at us, pen in the air. "This is a lot of hours. Are you sure you're up for it?"

This was the moment I had been waiting for. I tensed, preparing for combat. Did this mean she thought we had asked for more than we needed? Was she going to try to take something away? I launched back into our speech, more vehemently this time, explaining again why every service we had requested was essential. But not very far into it, I started to see that her question was genuine. For the first time, it struck me that these services weren't only for Henry. Early intervention is intended to serve the family, as well as the child. The therapists would be coming into my home and I would need to be present as they worked with my baby. I would have to follow through on the exercises they practiced with him.

Again, I nodded eagerly in agreement. But as I signed the paperwork, I suddenly wasn't at all sure that I wanted everything I had so vigorously demanded just a few minutes before. The mother of any two-month-old baby quickly learns that her life is not her own, a lesson Noah had taught me well. But early intervention took caregiving to a new level. Instead of simply whiling away my parental leave getting to know my new baby, I would spend days filled with doctor's appointments, therapy sessions, family training, and follow-through "homework." As I rode home in a taxi, I thumbed through my file of xeroxed documents. Henry slept next to me in his car seat, looking comfortable and untroubled. I wondered whether I was the kind of person who would sacrifice everything for my baby, and whether I would need to find out.

Early Intervention

EARLY INTERVENTION THREATENED the charmed life I had built for myself. Although I had a large office at the university, I had always preferred to work at home. When I started my life as an assistant professor, I quickly found campus to be a place of unpredictable hazards. I had a book to write, and my attention was constantly undermined by chatty office staff and senior colleagues trying to draw me into feuds that had started back when I was in high school. Undergraduates wanted me to hang out after office hours, advise the student vegetarian house, or judge the bad poetry contest. Committee work seemed to be doled out to the first person within view. I realized that my chances for professional survival would improve dramatically if I stayed at home, where I could work in pajamas and screen my calls, surrounded by piles of books and notes.

When we moved to New York, Jon and I designated one of the two bedrooms in our generous faculty apartment as my office. It was dark and cluttered, but I knew where everything was. After Jon left in the morning, I had the apartment to myself. My ability to work depended on being perfectly alone for long stretches of time, the stillness of our home punctuated by the noise of people and traffic on the street outside. Sharing that space with one child had taken some getting used to. The apartment we bought just before Noah was born still had only two bedrooms, and Noah lived in the one that would have been my office. I couldn't stop myself from imagining what it would be like to write in his big sunny room, my research spread out in the space that now held a crib, a changing table, and growing numbers of brightly colored plastic toys. Instead, I became quite good at reading and writing in bed, a mess of papers and books spread on the floor beside me.

I had sent my second book manuscript to press less than a week before Henry was born. Like so much in my life, everything was impeccably planned. I would turn in my final grades, give birth, spend four to six weeks of uninterrupted time with my new baby, then have the rest of my parental leave to complete the tedious work of copy-editing, proofreading, and indexing the manuscript, all of which would be done while he was sleeping. By the next spring, my second book would be published.

I hadn't anticipated early intervention coming into the picture. Just days after Henry's services were approved, the therapists started to arrive. Our life had to be structured around his appointments. I had purposefully chosen a career that didn't require me to manage other people. Suddenly, I was in charge of finding, scheduling, and inter-acting with an entire staff of caregivers. I was good at organization, but dealing with the human element—the quirks, needs, and short-comings of Henry's team—made me frustrated and impatient.

Early intervention works on the assumption that patterns of learning and behavior established during the first years of life will dramatically affect the subsequent rate and quality of a child's devel-opment. Whereas once intelligence was seen as a static quantity fixed within the individual at birth, early intervention is premised on the belief that it can be nurtured and developed, along with the muscles of the body. In fact, the two are closely related. Strengthening the body enough so that a child can play and explore the environment is essential for cognitive and emotional growth. The disciplines represented by Henry's team—physical and occupational therapy, special education, feeding, speech, and language—were intended to address the domains where he would experience the greatest developmental delays. But early intervention wasn't just about Henry. It recognized that children are part of families who also need education and support. Each therapist had sessions reserved for "family training" to update us on their progress and give us ways of building on their work with Henry. We also had weekly visits from a social worker whose entire job was to promote our happiness and well-being. Several times a year we were entitled to a team meeting where all of the therapists assembled to discuss Henry's needs and accomplishments.

Until Henry was born, I had never heard of early intervention, although I had devoted my career to studying the history of people with disabilities. I knew that before the era of modern medicine, disability was nothing out of the ordinary. Nearly every family was affected by disease, injury, or malnutrition. The disabled were cared for by their relatives and incorporated into the fabric of the communities where they lived. People with really spectacular disabilities could make a living by exhibiting themselves as freaks. At some point in the nineteenth century, the figure of the professional emerged. Doctors and scientists no longer wanted to share the limelight with the hucksters who organized carnivals and sideshows. They asserted their power and authority by developing specialized training, credentials, and professional societies. They laid claim to disability, turning bodies that had once been a source of wonder into medical cases.

Disabilities were named and documented, becoming problems to be cured or hidden from view. Powerful superintendents ensured the growth and stability of institutions devoted to housing the disabled, infirm, and mentally ill. Often these facilities were dirty and overcrowded, oriented less toward quality of life for their clients than toward removing them from the public eye.

My knowledge of this past made me appreciate the importance of the Americans with Disabilities Act (ADA), which guaranteed the civil rights of people with disabilities. The Education for All Handicapped Children Act of 1975 (EAHCA, renewed in 1990 as the Individuals with Disabilities Education Act [IDEA]) stipulated that children with disabilities were entitled to a "free and appropriate public education" in the "least restrictive environment." In 1986, the EAHCA was amended to include the provision of early intervention services to infants and toddlers with developmental delays. From birth to age three, children with disabilities would be issued an Individualized Family Service Plan (IFSP) like the one Henry had just received. When children graduated from early intervention, states were required to make appropriate public education available to them. Instead of being segregated and warehoused, children with disabilities would learn, to the greatest extent possible, alongside their nondisabled peers. And thanks to the ADA, as adults they would have the right to access public spaces, transportation, and places of work.

But I also wrote the book on freaks. The truth is, I was much more interested in the people who refused to be mainstreamed, continuing the tradition of the freak show by flaunting their differences for everyone to see. I loved visiting Sideshows by the Seashore at Coney Island and talking to its grizzled manager, Dick Zigun, about his attempts to preserve a dying American art form. I wrote enthusiastically about Jennifer Miller, a woman with a beard who is also an acrobat, juggler, and lesbian performance artist. And Coco the Killer Clown, a dwarf who covered his face with crudely applied grease paint, cracked jokes that nobody could understand, and made balloon shapes that looked nothing like animals. I was thrilled to find a little person who exhibited herself as "the World's Smallest Woman" in a trailer behind the Coney Island boardwalk. In high school I'd had a crush on a guy who wore a black T-shirt printed with the slogan "Why Be Normal?" I thought it was a great question.

I've always believed that the full integration of people with disabilities challenges our ideas about what counts as normal. As we confront the great variety of human embodiment and ability, we see that the world is a richer and more interesting place. But what I wanted most for my own son was for him to be as ordinary as possible. If he chose a career on stage someday, I wanted people to appreciate him because of his talents as a performer, not because he was different. I certainly didn't want people to judge him based on his appearance or on their preconceptions about his abilities.

Early intervention promised to give Henry the best possible chance at being included alongside his nondisabled peers. I learned that early intervention is particularly effective for children with Down syndrome, whose prospects for development improve dramatically with early and consistent therapy. Whereas a typical child knows to roll over at a certain stage, to babble at another, to stand up at yet a third, in a child with Down syndrome these instincts may be delayed by low muscle tone and sensory imbalances. Early intervention presumes that "muscle memory" is created by frequent repetition of each developmental goal. If a baby is rolled often enough, his muscles will learn to roll independently much sooner than if he is left to his own devices. So, too, with babbling and standing and the other developmental milestones a child is expected to reach between birth and the age of three. The goal of all of those half-hour therapy sessions was to build motor pathways that would guide Henry's muscles from one stage to another. The more quickly he was able to reach each milestone, the less delay he would experience in getting to the next stage of development.

Although early intervention is mandated by federal law, its resources are distributed at the state level. I had heard from friends in Colorado that a child might be put on a waiting list after she was qualified for services. I knew that families in New Jersey paid for their therapy on a sliding scale. At that time, the State of New York happened to have one of the best early intervention programs in the country. As soon as Henry's IFSP was approved, his therapy could begin. The state would charge my insurance company and then make up any of the costs that weren't covered by my plan. In cases where the child is uninsured, the entire amount is paid for by the state.

When we started early intervention, I discovered that my city is home to an army of therapists, almost all of them women, who spend their days traveling from home to home, lugging backpacks full of paperwork and equipment to treat their clients. For years I must have passed them on the sidewalk and shared seats with them on the bus, but Henry made them visible to me.

At first I would straighten up the apartment before each session, brushing my hair, changing out of my pajamas, and setting out soap and clean towels for the therapists to wash their hands. It took as much time to prepare for the therapists as to see them. On some days, I waited in dread for the sound of the doorbell, longing for the extended solitude of my former life. Sometimes, after a particularly sleepless night, I struggled to stay awake during Henry's sessions. Sometimes, I just didn't want to watch Henry's treatments or talk about his progress. And I found it hard to believe that a half-hour here and a half-hour there would really accomplish anything. Of course I dutifully completed all of the "homework" the therapists asked me to do in between sessions, rolling Henry this way and that, stimulating his hands and feet, passing black and white cards slowly in front of his eyes to help develop his tracking skills. I made notes about our activities on the "progress calendars" sent to us by his early intervention coordinator, and I kept after the therapists to write in a communication log for other members of the team to read. Even as I went about these tasks, there were many days when I wanted to scream with frustration as I thought of my colleagues teaching seminars, reading and writing, or jetting around the world to give talks and go to conferences. Worst of all were the times when I doubted whether anything I was doing would make a difference.

More often, I was glad to see the therapists, who brought a welcome sense of structure to our days. I got over my urge to clean and primp for them as I started to realize they had seen it all. They told stories of apartments packed to the roof with junk, floors covered so densely that there was no room to put the baby down, furniture smeared with unidentified sticky substances, strange odors, broken air conditioners, unflushed toilets, rats and cockroaches. They always had something positive to say about how Henry was doing, seeing progress in the tiniest change. This was a welcome contrast to his doctors, who focused so much attention on the impairments he had or might develop in the future. The therapists never talked as if Henry were disabled or suggested that there would be things he couldn't do. Giving myself over to them, I started to enjoy the rhythms of that strange, hot summer when everything changed.

Amara, the occupational therapist, worked with Henry on fine motor skills, core strength, and sensory awareness. She was a cheerful, birdlike person who shared my love for order and punctuality. She could gauge the precise time it would take her to get from one client to another so that not a minute of her day was wasted. While other therapists tended to be scheduled on the hour or half-hour, Amara's appointments were at times like 1:50 and 3:25. She came and went promptly, taking exactly five minutes to fill out her paperwork and leaving another minute or two for pleasantries on the way out. Amara was a strict Muslim who was born in Pakistan and raised in London, where she developed a delightful accent and an abiding hatred of peas. She observed more religious holidays than anyone I've ever known, although these rarely required her to miss work. It seemed like she was always fasting. There were many days when I knew she must have been hungry and parched, but she remained unerringly chipper during our sessions. She called Henry "love," and perched him sternly in various balancing poses while directing him to reach for a toy or his own feet. She designed exercises to improve his visual tracking, to help bring his floppy limbs toward the center of his body, and to develop upper-body stability. While she worked, she told stories about growing up in England, her family, and the training she was doing in her spare time. She was learning how to make occupational therapy equipment out of cardboard, techniques she hoped to introduce in the clinics she had visited while traveling in Africa.

Although we talked about many things, Amara's personal life remained mysterious. I knew she was in her early thirties, and she was clearly single. I wondered whether she might be a lesbian or just uninterested in a romantic relationship of any kind. Then one fall day she announced that she was going to get married and move back to England. On a recent trip to London she had been introduced to a man whom she planned to marry in January. She would rebuild her occupational therapy practice in Europe.

Amara exited with characteristic order and goodwill. She arranged to make up all of our missed sessions, and worked until the day before she left the country. I was happy for her, because she seemed pleased with the new course her life had taken. But I was sorry to see her go. She had been treating Henry since he was just eight weeks old and had become an important part of our lives. Saying goodbye to her was a reminder that treating children is a therapist's job. They might come to feel like fixtures in my household, and they might genuinely care for their clients, but therapists, like other working people, sometimes decide to move, retire, or change careers.

Henry's speech and feeding therapist was Jackie, a relentless optimist who found cause for hope in the same places where I found gloom and despair. "He's smiling," she said one day as Henry crumpled his face into what looked to me like a passing grimace. During another session, she was moved to tears when Henry lifted his arm as she got up to leave. "This is remarkable," she enthused. "Did you see that? Did you see what he just did? He waved goodbye." It didn't look like much to me. Henry spent a lot of time waving his arm. But I appreciated how much she cared about his progress. And sure enough, eventually Henry would wave and smile in a way that even I couldn't deny.

When it came to scheduling, Jackie was the antithesis of Amara. She rarely came at her scheduled times. Sometimes she was early, although more often she was late. She was always canceling or asking to reschedule. Jackie worked as a speech and language pathologist just a few blocks away at a local preschool. If she had a cancellation with one of her clients there, she would often show up at our door unannounced or call to say she was coming over. She seemed to think we were always at home waiting for her. As I struggled to squeeze my own work in around Henry's care, I was infuriated by her relaxed understanding of time. But as soon as I saw her with Henry, my anger dissolved. She found promise in his slightest accomplishment, and she knew just the right balance of strictness and fun to keep him in line. Henry loved Jackie, and he was willing to do things for her that he wouldn't do for anyone else. She inspired him to eat new things and make sounds. And it didn't matter to Henry whether she was late or seeing him on the wrong days.

Alison was our special educator, assigned to help Henry with play and social skills. She was an old-timer who had been involved with early intervention for decades, always pleasant, upbeat, and prompt. When her services had been offered to us at Henry's IFSP meeting, I had enthusiastically accepted. But for the first six months, I couldn't see any point to what she was doing. She read to Henry, sang him songs, and handed him toys while he looked blankly back at her from his recliner. Sometimes he was asleep when she came, and we would just talk. I liked her well enough, but as I sat there with my dozing baby, my head was filled with all the things I could be doing if she weren't there chatting with me.

Over time, Alison became an increasingly important part of Henry's therapy, and I came to love watching them together. She would sing "Five Little Monkeys" or "Wheels on the Bus," and he would pantomime the hand motions with delight, ending with an enthusiastic round of applause for himself. She taught Henry to play with dolls, brushing their hair, feeding them, and putting them to bed. They read books and did puzzles together. Once he could walk they formed a pretend band, marching around our living room singing, pounding on drums, and shaking tambourines. When Henry started preschool, it was clear that Alison had taught him valuable lessons about how to play and be a part of his classroom.

At the center of our group was Joy, Henry's physical therapist. Joy was the first name on the list Peggy had given us, and she had treated many children at BT over the years. It's easy to remember my initial impressions of her, because Joy is the kind of person who always looks reassuringly the same: brown hair, sensibly cut; jeans; comfort shoes; and a blue hooded sweatshirt. A down jacket or vest in cold weather.

That first day, she spread Henry on a blanket, moving him gently from side to side and singing while she worked. Her voice was an oasis of calm.

I know how her hands feel because she touched me once while Henry slept through a session. "Do you want to understand what I'm doing with him?" she asked.

I nodded.

She had me lie on the floor with my eyes closed. Her hands were strong, capable, and utterly persuasive as they rolled and bent my body into one pose after another. She talked as she worked, explaining exactly what she was doing.

When Joy wasn't singing during her sessions, we talked a lot. She told me about other children she had worked with. Some would never walk or talk. Many would spend their lives surrounded by medical equipment. One died of heart failure after a year.

Others had thrived on the foundations provided by early intervention. She had treated a girl with Down syndrome who was now in her second year of college. She told me about her aging mother and her dog, who suffered such intense fits of anxiety that one day he bit her to the bone. I found myself telling her things I hardly ever told anyone: about my mother's death, how hurt I was when Noah rejected me, my fears about being the parent of a child with disabilities.

Early Intervention

We talked about cooking, which I do a lot in times of crisis. During the first year of Henry's life, when I never managed to sleep enough and often went days without a shower, I did more baking than ever. In July a friend gave us an enormous bag of zucchini. Since nobody in my family likes zucchini, I made it into a chocolate cake. Using her favorite word of approval, Joy pronounced it "amazing," and I baked it nearly every week that summer. I would cut a big hunk and leave it wrapped in foil for her to take at the end of her sessions.

Joy seemed to think the world of Henry and to appreciate his smallest accomplishments. At some point in every session she would give him her highest compliment: "He's such a hard worker." One day she sat back after Henry had endured twenty minutes of rolling without complaint and told me, "You are blessed."

Although I don't usually think in such terms, at that moment I believed I was.

Joy was incredibly strong. I discovered this when she tried to teach me to do Henry's exercises. I watched her roll him onto his side, tuck his legs into position, and bring him up to sit. It looked easy enough. Henry weighed less than twenty pounds, and he allowed himself to be guided by Joy's hands. Everything changed when my turn came. He must have sensed an absence of authority in my touch because he immediately began to fuss and squirm, locking his legs out straight so that it was impossible for me to bend them into position. The harder I tried, the more he resisted. I broke into a sweat as I struggled to coordinate his arms, legs, and torso. "Can you show me one more time?" I panted.

As soon as Joy touched him, Henry got quiet, sensing that she was in charge. She brought him easily to sit. "I'll write this down as your homework," she offered.

Early Intervention

Once the sitting exercise became homework, I was determined to get it right. I put a mat on the floor by my side of the bed, and we practiced first thing in the morning, when Henry was in his most agreeable mood. I learned that the trick was to move quickly, getting him into position before he knew what was happening. Soon enough I was able to do the sitting exercise beautifully. Best of all, Joy told me I was "amazing."

By the time the season of chocolate zucchini cake returned, Henry wasn't so pliable. He had developed a strong will, and his own ideas about what his body should be doing. He started to move around with a lurching, uneven crawl that Joy viewed with disapproval. She said it would make his later motor development imbalanced. We had to stop it, and stop it now. I was supposed to crawl along behind him and force him onto all fours.

Henry had other ideas. As soon as I got near, he made his displeasure known with loud cries of rage. When I touched his leg, he collapsed onto his stomach and slithered away, only to sit up just out of my reach and begin the lopsided crawl all over again. Henry's newfound rebellion made sessions with Joy excruciating. She would get him onto his hands and knees, holding his hips and inching one leg forward at a time while he screamed in protest. My job was to distract him. After half an hour of singing, coaxing, imploring, and offering all of the gadgets and toys I could think of, I was exhausted.

Joy had always struck me as someone who had seen it all. But Henry's protests clearly upset her. "Maybe he's not feeling well," she would say time and again. "He isn't acting like himself. Could he be tired?"

I found these comments exasperating, since Henry seemed equally resistant, regardless of whether he was sick or well, tired or rested. Joy was the therapist, and she should know how to solve the problem.

Early Intervention

By that time, we were planning for Henry to start daycare in the fall. I wondered whether it would be better for him to split his time between Joy, who would treat him at school, and a second physical therapist, who would work with him at home. I thought maybe a new physical therapist could shake him out of the funk he seemed to be in with Joy.

Since I was used to getting Joy's advice about almost everything, I asked her what she thought about this idea.

She responded with a long silence. "Sure that's fine," she said finally, looking down as she gathered her things together. "If that's what you want."

She left so quickly that she forgot to take the piece of chocolate zucchini cake I had wrapped for her.

When I talked to her the next morning, I started to wonder whether she had forgotten the cake or deliberately left it behind. A metaphor for our imploding relationship. At the beginning of her session with Henry, I asked her about a therapist named Lisa, who had been recommended by a friend. Of course it was Joy's opinion about Lisa that mattered most to me. She told me she had never heard of Lisa. "I'm sure she's fine," she told me, shortly. "And since you want a change, you should start with her as soon as possible."

"But I don't think she'll be available on such short notice," I said, surprised. "I thought we were planning for the fall."

"It'll be fine," she said flatly. "Just call her and tell her you need someone right away."

She picked Henry up and started to work with him. He began to wail, clearly putting an end to the conversation. I tried to distract him, but suddenly I felt deflated, stupid. I could hear my own tuneless singing, my pathetic attempts to be funny and dramatic. Noah ran into the room naked from the waist down and grabbed the toy I was waving. I became uncomfortably aware of the chaos in our apartment, the crumbs in the rug just inches from Joy's face, a dirty coffee cup left out from earlier that morning.

What had I done? I wondered. Joy had agreed that Henry should see a second therapist in the fall, but why did she seem so eager to get rid of us now? Was working with us so unbearable that she couldn't wait another three months? Was Henry untreatable? Did I talk too much during her sessions? Maybe I didn't try hard enough? Joy was always telling me I was too negative. Had my complaining finally gotten to her?

After the conversation about Lisa, I sent Joy an email asking why she wanted to stop treating Henry so suddenly. Was her decision based on a clinical opinion? Was it something we had done? If so, shouldn't we know about it so that we could avoid doing it in the future? She wrote back with terse, one-word replies. No, no, and no. "You said you wanted a change so I think now is the time."

Her words stayed with me. I didn't remember saying I wanted a change. I had asked her opinion about whether a change—three months down the road—would be appropriate. I felt misunderstood. I started to feel resentful.

After a few sleepless nights, I saw things differently. Could it be that Joy felt we were dumping her? Was she acting so cold and terse because she had been hurt by us? Joy had been our rock. She had spent hours working with our baby to make him strong. When he took his first steps, it would be because his muscles remembered her guiding touch. What would our lives be like without Joy? Why did we want another therapist anyway? If I asked her to stay, would she agree?

I got up the next morning chagrined but determined. I would tell Joy I had made a terrible mistake. There had been a misunderstanding.

Early Intervention

We had never wanted anyone else. I had asked an innocent question, and things had very quickly gotten out of control. Would she stay with us? Would she take on the extra sessions at home and also see Henry at school? Would that be enough?

When she arrived, I launched nervously into my prepared speech. Halfway through, Joy smiled and said of course she would stay.

And that was it. Henry didn't cry at all during his session, and she got him to crawl—symmetrically, on all fours—from the living room to the kitchen.

The next day, he made up for lost time by screaming louder than ever. I sang and made funny noises. Noah ran through the room naked. We were about to go away for the weekend, and I told Joy that I dreaded being trapped in a cabin in the rain with two kids. She told me to stop being so negative.

And just like that, everything was back to normal.

I've done my reading, and I've seen the evidence that shows what a tremendous difference therapy makes in the development of young children with Down syndrome. There were times when Henry's therapists made me angry and exasperated and bored. I'll never know what his progress would have been like without them. But I'm absolutely convinced that they made a difference. Even more important, they gave me a sense of hope and purpose. As they pushed Henry from one goal to another, they always took time to praise what he could already do. Now that he can walk and talk on his own, I like to think that ingrained in Henry's muscles are the memories of all the rolling and pushing up and balancing and lifting that got him there, but also the touch of the many people who helped him along the way.

Choices

WHEN HENRY WAS TEN MONTHS OLD, I took him to a baby shower for some colleagues who live downtown. They are both second-generation academics, and I knew many of the guests would be professors. Still, I wasn't prepared to be greeted at the door by Rayna Rapp, an anthropology professor at New York University and author of a book on prenatal testing that happened to be sitting on my bedside table at home. A friend had given it to me after Henry was born, and I was just getting around to reading it. I was riveted by the introduction, where Rapp writes about her decision to have a late-term abortion after an amniocentesis showed that the fetus she was carrying had Down syndrome. She and her husband wanted a child but couldn't imagine raising one with a disability that might have a devastating impact on their lives. The abortion was traumatic, and Rapp describes the feeling of loss that stayed with her long after her body had returned to its prepregnancy shape. She spent the next decade doing fieldwork with doctors, genetic counselors, expectant parents, and the parents of children with genetic disabilities to learn more about how prenatal testing was changing the meaning of pregnancy and parenthood in America. The end product was the smart and thoughtful book I was reading.

As soon as I realized who had opened the door, my mind started to whirl. Reading Rapp's book was an intense experience. One minute I would be in tears, the next minute I was nodding vigorously in agreement, juggling much stronger emotions than I was used to feeling toward an academic book. It was helping to focus some of the questions about genetics and prenatal testing that had been buzzing around in my head since Henry's birth, but I wasn't ready to discuss them with the author herself. A baby shower seemed like a particularly inopportune place for a meeting like this. After all, this was supposed to be a celebration of new life coming into the world, not a time to think about all the things that could go wrong in the process.

Standing on the welcome mat of that stylish apartment in Chelsea, Henry dangling from my chest in his baby carrier, I was conscious of the choices that had led to his birth. Unlike Rayna Rapp, I never had an amniocentesis.

I know.

This is shockingly risky behavior on the part of an ambitious, overeducated, overachieving person like myself. Amnio was made for people like me, women with a deep need for order and control and perfection. Women who strongly believe in the right to abortion. Technology was supposed to liberate the woman who needs to know she will never have to be the mother of a child like Henry.

So what the hell was I thinking?

The first time around, I did exactly what was expected. When I was pregnant with Noah, I wanted to know everything. I was thirty-six, a year beyond the age when the chances of having a baby with Down syndrome and other genetic conditions start to increase significantly, making me a prime candidate for an amnio. My obstetrician, Dr. Lewis, presented us with a full range of options: we could start with a noninvasive test called the "fully integrated screen," a combination of ultrasound and bloodwork to predict the likelihood of genetic abnormalities. The screen can tell you whether your fetus has a one-in-twenty or a one–in–one thousand chance of having a genetic anomaly. But it can't give you a definitive diagnosis. We could also go directly to amnio. Or we could do no testing at all. I sensed that she was trying her best to be impartial, but that she also had opinions. From the way she described each of our choices, it seemed she preferred that we avoid invasive testing unless earlier screenings showed that something might be amiss.

I agreed to start with the screen. When the results came in, they predicted less than a one–in–three thousand chance of having a baby with a genetic condition. Dr. Lewis clearly thought that was good enough. She told me she saw no reason for the riskier procedure when the screenings said I was no more likely to have a baby with a genetic disease than a woman in her twenties. I disagreed. The screen said it was unlikely that our fetus had a genetic condition. *Unlikely*, but not impossible. The perfectionist in me needed to know. I was quite sure that if I skipped the test, I would spend the next six months worrying about whether my baby's genes were healthy. That couldn't be good for his health, or mine. The only way to get the information with absolute certainty was to have an amnio. But another part of me was the girl without a mother. I already felt an intense urge to protect the little bundle of cells growing inside of me. I was terrified that something would go wrong and the amnio would damage our otherwise perfectly developing child.

I'm not a dreamer. I hardly ever remember my dreams, and when I do, they're usually tediously literal reenactments of my daily life: I'm going to the market, teaching a class, having office hours. But the night before the amnio, I dreamed I was driving on a winding mountain road. Michael Bérubé and Janet Lyon were in the back seat of the car. That's all I remember. I sat up in a panic and shook Jon awake. What could this mean? Obviously they were there as the parents of Jamie, who has Down syndrome. I knew from reading Michael's book that he and Janet had chosen not to have an amnio. Jamie's birth came as a complete surprise at the end of an uneventful pregnancy. What were they doing in my dream? Had they appeared to warn me not to go ahead with the test? Or were they there to tell me that it was okay, to show their understanding that my choices might be different from theirs?

I decided they were there to support me, and I had the test. It hurt when the doctor inserted the needle into my abdomen. I remember the experience vividly, the worn, green sweatpants I was wearing, the darkened room, the ultrasound, the doctor telling me that, in the unlikely event that the procedure caused the amniotic sac to break, there would be no way to save the fetus. As the fluid was drawn, I had a nauseating feeling of something vital being sucked out of my body. But my fear that the baby would be hurt was worse than the physical pain. And long after I got the news that our baby was genetically normal, I was still afraid that somehow I had damaged him. The screenings suggested he was fine, but I had put him at risk nonetheless.

As soon as I got pregnant again, I started to worry about prenatal testing. I don't know whether it was anxiety or just morning sickness that made me so nauseated at the thought of that needle. This time, the fully integrated screen revealed a one–in–two thousand chance of Down syndrome. At age thirty-eight, those were very good odds. Statistically, I was just as likely to die by falling in the shower, and far more likely to date a millionaire, write a *New York Times* best seller, or catch a ball at a major league baseball game.

More important, this time around Jon and I knew a lot more about ourselves as parents. We knew we didn't love Noah because he had good genes. Wonderful as he was, we also knew he wasn't perfect. No prenatal test can guarantee a perfect child, or even a perfectly healthy one.

I learned that lesson through experience. A few months after Noah was born, I got to know Rose, whose daughter Abigail was almost exactly Noah's age. Rose's prenatal testing had been completely normal, but Abigail wasn't. At birth, she was weak and had trouble feeding. She was such an irritable baby that Rose was often exhausted. It was hard to get Abigail to take naps, and when she did, her sleep was fitful and irregular. She didn't explore things with her mouth the way typical babies do, and she rejected food of all tastes and textures. At one stage she would eat only blueberries and Pop Tarts, which Rose had allowed her to try in a fit of desperation. At another she would eat round tortilla chips but not triangles. By the time she was one, any change in her environment sent her into uncontrollable tantrums. When she finally learned to sit up—months after Noah and other kids her age—she started to rock and flap her arms. At eighteen months, she was diagnosed with pervasive developmental disorder, which meant a combination of developmental delays and behavior on the autism spectrum. Rose and her husband immediately put Abigail on an intense regimen of therapy. They saw one doctor after another, hoping that someone could cure their child. One recommended a complete blood transfusion; another force-feeding. They started to think of everything Abigail did, including play and sleep, in terms of "work." Rose saw disability everywhere, in the quirks and moods of everybody else's children. Finally, I got so tired of hearing her diagnose Noah with one disorder or another that I stopped seeing her. But our brief friendship made me realize that there is no prenatal test to

Choices

guarantee a perfectly normal baby. Most things that will go wrong with your child happen after birth.

With this in mind, Jon and I made different choices the second time around. Our screening revealed that we had a pretty good chance of giving birth to a completely typical baby. But people do get struck by lightning. Somebody wins the lottery. And we got Henry. I call him my miracle child, the one who beat the odds.

STANDING THERE IN THE DOORWAY with Rayna Rapp, I felt like I was part of a bad metaphor. Together, we embodied all of the unknowns expectant parents just can't think about. It turned out she was an old friend of the pregnant mother's family. I introduced myself and told her that I admired her work. She was appreciative and kind, and we chatted briefly about the difficulties of juggling parenthood and an academic career. I told her I was struggling to finish my second book.

"I can imagine how hard it is," she nodded, looking at Henry. "I'm sure you have a lot going on."

She invited me to get something to eat, took my coat, and that was the end of our conversation. I knew Henry wasn't the first person with Down syndrome she had run into over the years. She writes about doing fieldwork with a local Down syndrome parent support group and the National Down Syndrome Society. Even though we had spoken only briefly, I felt we had communicated in a profound and respectful way about the very different choices each of us had made. She had opted not to continue her pregnancy; I had made choices that allowed me to avoid such painful decisions. I knew I appreciated her choices, and I believed she did mine.

My chance meeting with Rayna Rapp also left me thinking about the confusing and contradictory messages that surround the notion of reproductive choice in our culture. At the time Rapp decided to have her abortion in 1983, there were far fewer resources for the parents of a child with Down syndrome. Just a year earlier, an infant known as Baby Doe was born in Indiana. She had deformities of the esophagus that would be fatal without surgical intervention. She also had Down syndrome. Her parents declined medical treatment and allowed her to die. While this was an extreme case, it was generally true that babies and children with Down syndrome simply didn't receive adequate medical treatment. Life expectancy was little more than twenty-one years. Although the Education for All Handicapped Children Act had been in place since 1975, opportunities for developmental therapy and educational inclusion varied greatly from state to state. Many people with Down syndrome still lived in institutions where nobody had to see them or acknowledge that they even existed. There were no publicly visible models of successful inclusion. It's no wonder Rapp and her husband believed their lives might be devastated by caring for a disabled child.

Times had changed. A person with Down syndrome can now expect to live more than fifty years, thanks to better health care and a more accommodating social environment. People with Down syndrome have gained a new visibility, if you know where to look. Since Henry was born, I had been making a scrapbook that I imagined reading with him when he got old enough to appreciate it. On the first page was one of my prize possessions, a signed publicity photo of Chris Burke, the actor with Down syndrome who starred on the hit TV show *Life Goes On*. He's also an author and a musician with his own band. I collected articles about Lauren Potter, who had a recurring role on the popular TV show *Glee*; Pablo Pineda, who won the best actor award at the 2009 San Sebastian film festival for his role in the Spanish film *Yo también* [*Me, Too*]; and Andrea Friedman, who sparked controversy for her self-deprecating voice-over on the animated TV series *Family Guy*. There were newspaper stories about Karen Gaffney, a world-class swimmer and president of her own nonprofit organization; Casey Deegan, who skydives with his father; Tim Harris, who owns and operates a restaurant in Albuquerque; and Kristin Pass, who was elected homecoming queen at Aledo High School in Texas. There was a flier from a New York gallery opening where the work of Haile King Rubie, Ashlee Birckhead, Bernadette Resha, and other artists with Down syndrome was exhibited. I also collected books by people with Down syndrome, like the autobiographical *The World of Nigel Hunt*, Burke's *A Special Kind of Hero*, and Jason Kingsley and Mitchell Levitz's *Count Us In*, and by parents like George Estreich and, of course, Michael Bérubé. The self-advocacy movement had empowered people with intellectual disabilities to speak and act on their own behalf. The year 2006 marked the first celebration of World Down Syndrome Day, which was observed by countries including the United States, Canada, Mexico, Japan, Singapore, Brazil, Saudi Arabia, Switzerland, Turkey, Kenya, and New Zealand. These stories of success and possibility made me think again about John Langdon Down and the imperative to "aim high enough." Maybe it was time to reclaim the best of his legacy, while forgetting about his more predictably Victorian urges toward classification and hierarchy. Maybe it was time to stop doubting the capability of people with Down syndrome and to look instead at what they had accomplished when given the right environment and opportunities. The scrapbook said it all. I saw it as my guarantee that Henry would grow up in a very different world than he would have if he had been born even twenty years earlier.

But less uplifting change was also reconfiguring the field of genetics. In 2003 scientists finished mapping the genes that make up human DNA. New genetic markers for diseases and disabilities were discovered every day. On the horizon were gene therapies that promised to cure or prevent hereditary diseases. The explosion in genetic information had come in like a stealth bomb, with virtually no public conversation or debate about what purpose it was intended to serve. I had heard geneticists describe their work as opening a Pandora's box. The science was racing ahead without any collective agreement—let alone policies or legislation—about how to use it or when it should be regulated. Questions about who owns our genetic information and what should be done with it seemed sure to be among the most hotly debated topics of the next decades.

Genetic testing to identify chromosomal abnormalities has become a routine aspect of pregnancy in the United States and throughout the Western world. Soon it will be possible to detect any number of features in a developing fetus, including hair and eye color, potential height, weight, and intelligence. Many people believe there is an ethical difference between tests that would identify such "designer" genetic characteristics, and those intended to determine the health of the fetus. But how do we decide what counts as health and what constitutes a disease? What about genetically transmitted diseases like breast cancer or Huntington's that may not manifest for decades? What about women who abort based on the sex of an otherwise healthy fetus? Amniocentesis already has the capacity to detect a wide number of conditions, ranging from the potentially insignificant (some forms of sex chromosome anomalies) to the universally fatal (Tay Sachs, anencephaly, Trisomies 13 and 18). Rapp writes that pregnant women increasingly find themselves in the position of moral gatekeepers who are forced to make decisions about which genetic conditions are compatible with life and which should warrant termination. It's hard to imagine otherwise in a free, democratic society in which women can and should have exclusive control over their bodies.

At the same time, we might well speculate about how those decisions would be affected by more accurate, less biased information about genetic disabilities.

One area where the information is woefully inadequate is in explaining what it means to know that your fetus will be born with a nonlethal condition like Down syndrome, spina bifida, or Turner's syndrome. The amnio reveals the genetic makeup of your fetus. That's all. It can't tell you that your baby will be perfect, or even perfectly normal. It can't predict how a chromosomal anomaly will affect the health and developmental capacities of any given individual. It certainly can't tell prospective parents what it will be like to raise a child with a disability or anything about the person that baby will become.

I had thought a lot about what it would have meant for Jon and me to have had Henry's genetic information before he was born. We would have known that he had one more chromosome than his brother. This information would have led us to expect him to have low muscle tone, to be slower to walk and talk, and to be smaller than other children his age. But none of that gets me to the essence of Henry. I couldn't have known about his great sense of humor or the sound of his infectious laugh. Or the smell of his hair. The delight he gets from singing along with music or pouring bathwater from one cup to another. His unflagging admiration for his big brother. His weight on my lap when we're reading a book together. That he loves to walk around with a puppet on each hand, making them talk to each other in animated gibberish. Or the way he can groove on ice cream, retreating into some inner zone of joy as he sticks his face deep into the cone. There is no genetic test to tell me about the thousand inchoate qualities that made my son the person he was.

All the attention and resources poured into prenatal testing guaranteed that Henry's world was also a place where health care professionals often saw him as a failure of medical science. Our eye doctor said as much when she used him to teach a lesson about the unreliability of prenatal screening. "We're seeing more babies born with Down syndrome," she said to her resident, as I sat in her office with Henry on my lap. "It's because these tests tend to yield false negatives." At the time I was too stunned to speak. I couldn't believe she would use me to tell a story about science gone awry. And while I was sitting right there in front of her, no less. Later, I sent her a letter saying how much I resented hearing my baby described as a mistake. She was chagrined. "It's just that doctors want everything to be perfect," she told me apologetically. Enough said. The implication was, of course, that Henry wasn't perfect. Which he wasn't. Then again, who is?

Of course it wasn't just doctors. In the circles I frequented, where intelligence and intellectual achievement are valued above all else, we talked a lot about our appreciation for diversity. But that appreciation didn't usually extend to intellectual disability or what some now call neurodiversity. The evidence is there in the glossy college brochures that illustrate diversity by picturing students of many different races and nationalities. Where are the students in wheelchairs, the guide dogs, and the sign interpreters? It was even harder to imagine a place at the university for students who could not meet the standards of productivity, brilliance, and articulacy so valued by my profession. We live in a society that equates personhood with self-possession, autonomy, and the ability to reason. Those who lack such qualities have often been excluded from the rights and responsibilities of citizenship, and even deemed to be less than human. I wondered whether my friends and colleagues would recognize the value of a child who was slower, less capable, and more dependent.

On hearing the news of Henry's birth, more than one friend responded by asking how this could have happened to me. "Didn't you get tested?" a well-known scholar of disability studies questioned me incredulously as we stood in the middle of a cocktail party. This from someone who has devoted his career to challenging cultural norms of ability and perfection. Or the mom at preschool who asked, the first time we met, whether I "knew about Henry" before he was born. "No," I wanted to snap at her. "It was the darnedest thing. I couldn't figure out why I was getting so fat!" Babies like Henry simply aren't born to successful, overeducated parents like us. Something must have gone terribly wrong. Many people seemed to believe that knowing what that something was would help to ensure it would never happen to them.

I found those questions irritating, but I also understood them. A few years ago I would have been the one doing the asking. We live in a world where a baby like Henry demands a story. I should know that better than anyone. I'm a literary critic, and I study narrative for a living. I try to imagine what it would be like if Henry's story and mine had unfolded differently. What if I had made different choices? Taken more tests? I try, but I've never been able to do it. As Jon said matter-of-factly soon after Henry was born, "It happened to us." And so, on that fall afternoon in Chelsea, I stepped into the party with Henry clutched to my chest, ready to congratulate my friends.

Visiting the Front Lines

BUMPING INTO RAYNA RAPP MADE me aware of the prominent place genetics had come to occupy in our lives. Few people think much about genetics, even as the science races ahead, perfecting techniques for cloning, gene therapy, and detection of disease and disability. But for my family, a small error in cell division changed all of that.

It started the morning after Henry was born, when a resident from the genetics department knocked tentatively at the door of my hospital room. She wanted to complete a pedigree, a standard family history that traces a patient's genetic ancestry. I tried not to wince near the end, when she asked whether Jon and I could be related. This is a sensitive question when you're married to someone from the South, a place that, in the minds of New Yorkers, conjures up images of freakish inbreds like the hillbillies in the movie *Deliverance*. Even more sensitive when there's some truth behind the clichés. Jon's grandparents, the ones who were good country people from Appalachia, were distant cousins on both sides. Putting that aside, I could say with absolute certainty that never before had the genetic material of the Scots-Irish peasants in Jon's family tree encountered the genetic material of the eastern European peasants in mine. Absolutely no chance. And what did it matter? Down syndrome has nothing to do with inbreeding and is rarely hereditary. It's an accident that happens at the moment of conception, except in unusual cases called translocation, where the extra twenty-first chromosome lies latent in somebody's genes even before the meeting of sperm and egg.

"My son has Down syndrome, for Pete's sake," I wanted to snap at her. But I held my tongue. I knew that she was just doing her job, which required her to ask the same questions of everybody.

After we finished the questionnaire, she told me we could do a genetic analysis to confirm that Henry had Down syndrome. It would take about two weeks to get the results. I asked her whether she thought there was any chance the doctors could have made a mistake. Had she ever heard of a case like Henry's where Down syndrome was suspected but not confirmed?

She thought for a moment. "Once," she said. "It turned out that a lot of the physical features we associate with Down syndrome ran in the family. When we saw them together, we realized the baby looked just like its relatives."

When I looked at the infant Henry, I saw nothing of myself or anyone else in our family. Then again, he had the pinched, angry red look of all newborn babies. I reminded myself that I had never known an infant to look anything like its relatives, or even the baby it would become. I clung to this as if it were the truth. Somewhere deep inside, I held onto the faint hope that there had been a mistake. The resident told us it was possible Henry's analysis would reveal mosaicism, a rare condition in which some genes have the extra twenty-first chromosome that causes Down syndrome and others don't. In cases of mosaicism, symptoms of Down syndrome are typically milder, and some parts of the body aren't affected at all.

When I called back two weeks later, the results were as we had expected. There had been no mistake. Henry had Trisomy 21. No mosaic. Just your garden-variety Down syndrome. The resident suggested that we should make an appointment to see her mentor, the hospital's head geneticist, Dr. Marburg.

Dr. Marburg? I wasn't sure I had heard her right. Wasn't that a nasty tropical disease? I asked her to repeat the name. "Dr. Mar*bourne*," she said more clearly, spelling it out. She offered to make the appointment for us. We could come back when Henry was six months old. I didn't see what harm could come of it, so I agreed.

IN PRIVATE, I CONTINUED to call him Dr. Marburg. On the day of our appointment, I realized I had already met the great doctor. He was the one who gathered his residents around Henry's incubator, putting him on display like a sideshow freak.

If he remembered us, he didn't show it. He asked us to strip Henry down to his diaper for a physical exam. While we busied ourselves with the undressing, he skimmed through the notes his assistant had taken about Henry's health and development. He put Henry on the scale, measured his head size and length, nodding and muttering softly to himself. When he was satisfied, he stepped back. Henry appeared to be developing well, he told us. There were no major health problems, he was growing, and, despite his muscle weakness, his fine and gross motor skills seemed to be advancing nicely.

"The greatest area of concern is his speech," the doctor told us. "That's where these people often experience significant delays. Some of them do end up talking. Others don't. They may use sign language or computers to help them communicate. In this case, we'll just have to wait and see. I'd like you to bring him back in six months."

None of this was the least bit surprising. We already knew Henry was in good health. He spent so much time with doctors and therapists that not a cell on his body wasn't being tracked by someone. I didn't like the way the doctor said "these people," and I didn't really see the point of coming back, but I let his assistant make us another appointment. Maybe somewhere down the line, a geneticist would see something in Henry that others had overlooked. What was the harm? It seemed to me that the more medical attention he had, the better off he would be.

Later, I would change my mind. We saw Dr. Marburg two more times, once just after Henry's first birthday and again at eighteen months. Jon couldn't miss work on the day of our last appointment, so Henry and I went without him. The doctor greeted us as he came into the room, trailed by a younger man and a woman whom he introduced as medical residents.

He asked me to undress Henry and sit with him on my lap. Then he turned his attention to the residents. "Please recite the features."

They gazed at him uncomfortably. Then they looked at us. There was a long silence. "The eyes," the man said hesitantly.

"What about the eyes?" the doctor quizzed him.

"The epicanthal folds," the man replied. "There's some extra skin and the eyes are slanted upward at the corners."

"Yes, good. What else?"

"The mouth," the man offered. "Low muscle tone. And his ears are small."

"Correct," said Dr. Marburg, turning back to Henry. "You should also note that his hair is thin, the abnormally shallow bridge of the nose, and the protruding belly, which is an effect of hypotonia. Oh, and look at this." He picked up Henry's hand. "Look at the tip of his little finger. It's slightly crooked."

I perched on my seat, silent and incredulous. It was 2009. We were sitting in the office of a respected hospital in New York City, but this felt too much like a freak show, with Henry and me as the main attraction. In the nineteenth century, when the lines between medicine and show business were fuzzier, freak shows often made a place for doctors. They lent an aura of seriousness and authority to the enterprise. In return, freak shows provided doctors with a steady stream of medical curiosities to examine and study. As long as a doctor was present, the freak could be poked and prodded, discussed and exposed, all in the name of science. Middle-class audiences felt authorized to stare and question, because they were doing it for educational purposes.

Wading through the archives, I loved finding those rare moments when freaks declared that enough was enough by talking back or lashing out at the experts onstage. In those bursts of rebellion, freaks remind us that they have needs and feelings, just like everybody else. I liked to think that seeing those outbursts would have helped the audience to acknowledge the person on display as a fellow human being.

The appointment with Dr. Marburg could have been my moment. But I missed my cue. I'm the shy girl, remember? The one who spent her childhood in the corner reading a book? There would be no outburst. I just sat there mortified, looking down at Henry and waiting for the moment to pass. I know grand rounds are a ritual of medical education. I know doctors need to see patients and talk about their symptoms in order to learn how to treat them. But Henry wasn't sick. There were no symptoms. No prognosis. No treatment was being prescribed. His genes had already been examined, his condition identified. Not once had this doctor offered a new insight about my son's health or development.

It was then that I thought I understood why the doctor kept inviting us back. It wasn't that he had anything to contribute to Henry's care. It was because he saw Henry as a curiosity. Back in the days before amniocentesis, geneticists used to see plenty of cases of Down syndrome. But once genetic testing became commonplace, babies with Down syndrome were fewer and farther between. I had heard more than one doctor remark on this trend. From a geneticist's point of view Down syndrome is interesting. It's far more complicated than a congenital disease like cystic fibrosis, which involves just a single gene mutation. While doctors may have opportunities to study the medically fragile kids with Down syndrome who spend their lives in and around hospitals, a healthy child like Henry was harder to come by.

The residents lingered for a few minutes watching Henry play on the floor. They asked me about his development and his therapy program. They seemed charmed, and I felt like they were trying to make up for the way the doctor had thrust them on us. When they left, they thanked me for letting them observe our appointment. I thanked them for their time, knowing we wouldn't be back.

SOON AFTER OUR LAST VISIT with Dr. Marburg, I started to write. It was the only way I knew to make sense of what had happened in the months since Henry was born. At first my writing was private, an undisciplined jumble of thoughts and descriptions of things that had happened. There were already plenty of memoirs by the parents of children with Down syndrome, and I wasn't sure I had anything new to contribute. Reading them made me feel reassured that I wasn't alone. But I also had a more irrational feeling of violation when I saw just how much our experiences seemed to echo those of countless other families who had gone before. Writing became a way to claim those experiences as my own, to resist the sense that I was living out a story someone else had already written. But it was also about accepting our participation in a broader collective experience. The more I wrote, the more I realized I was speaking not just about Henry and me but about a whole class of people who, for much of human history, had been hidden from view. I started to see my writing not only as a way of capturing the particularities of my own experience but as a way to communicate with other parents and even to talk back to the doctors and researchers and anyone who went around spouting outdated and incorrect information about Down syndrome.

I showed an essay I had written about prenatal testing to some of the other moms I had come to know. It hit a nerve with my friend Colleen, who had had some unfortunate encounters with doctors after she received a prenatal diagnosis of Down syndrome and heart disease. As she struggled to accept the news and learn more about her son's prognosis, she also found herself repeatedly forced to justify her decision not to terminate the pregnancy. She found it devastating to meet one doctor after another who assumed that abortion would be the next logical step. Her son Aaron was born just a few weeks after Henry, and he needed cardiac surgery at two months. At the time, Colleen was too overwhelmed by caring for a newborn with Down syndrome and heart failure to think about talking back to the doctors, or anything that didn't have to do with surviving from one day to the next.

Two years later, Aaron was thriving and Colleen felt ready to talk about genetics. She remembered that, during her pregnancy, she had seen a geneticist, whose card sat forgotten in a drawer until my essay reminded her it was there. After making some calls, she managed to set up a meeting with a group of geneticists and genetic counselors at the hospital where Aaron was born. I agreed to go with her. I knew Colleen needed a chance to talk about her experiences with doctors and genetic counselors, and I admired her for going directly back to the source. At the same time, I wasn't sure what she hoped to accomplish, beyond an airing of grievances. I imagined they might listen politely, then try to get us out of there as soon as possible so that they could go back to work.

As it turned out, the geneticists were delighted to meet us, and we talked for more than two hours. Like Dr. Marburg, they worked in a hospital where they had very little access to parents of children with disabilities who weren't also gravely ill. Colleen and I gave them perspective on what it was like to live with a disability that wasn't all about illness and infirmity. I realized that there were geneticists who wanted to learn from our experiences instead of just writing us off as a tragic glitch in the system. When the meeting finally broke up, we resolved to find more opportunities for conversation.

THE FIRST WAS AN INVITATION to speak at Sarah Lawrence College, which is home to the oldest and most prestigious human genetics program in the country. Founded in 1969, it has trained half of the genetic counselors currently working in the United States. Caroline Lieber, the program's director, learned about Colleen and me from a student intern who had been sitting in on our meeting at the hospital. She asked us to come for two consecutive visits. The first would be a chance to tell our stories. On a second visit we would give a more structured presentation about how counselors could better serve the families of people with genetic disabilities.

I had never been to Sarah Lawrence, which turned out to fit perfectly with my image of a northeastern liberal arts college, with its gated driveway, charming stone buildings, and well-groomed lawns and hedges. I was used to giving academic talks, but I hadn't traveled much since Henry was born. As I stood in front of the room like so many others where I had lectured before, I was surprised at how nervous I felt. Always in the past I had spoken as a professor sharing my research with students and colleagues. Here I had been asked to speak as a parent, on a subject I knew through personal experience rather than professional authority. Our audience was mostly first- and second-year genetic counseling students, with a smattering of program faculty. They listened politely while we talked about genetic counseling, prenatal testing, and our new babies. They cooed with appreciation when we showed pictures of our little boys. And they asked thoughtful questions about how we thought they could do their jobs more effectively.

I had gone into this meeting thinking I might find resistance, even antagonism. I understood genetic counselors to be working for an industry bent on increasing the effectiveness and scope of genetic testing, with the goal of eliminating children like mine. Even if they tried to be impartial, I imagined that most counselors believed firmly in using genetic science to normalize, and possibly even improve, the quality of the human species. I was sure that none of them had ever met a person with a genetic disability. How could they counsel parents about what it would mean to have a condition they knew nothing about?

Once again, it turned out that I was pretty far off base. It was clear that these students had thought deeply about the ethical dilemmas of genetic counseling. Over the course of their program, they spent a lot of time learning how to support expectant parents of many different ethnic, religious, economic, and educational backgrounds. They believed it was essential to respect their clients' assumptions about child-rearing and family. They didn't go into the encounter thinking there was one right answer. Instead, they tried to help prospective parents make informed choices in keeping with their values and life plans. They understood the profound dilemmas genetic knowledge is unleashing on our culture and saw themselves as guides who could help people to navigate the coming barrage of information. Almost all of them had met at least one person with a genetic disability, and they saw that experience as an important part of their training. Their problem, they agreed, was access. As we had already learned, it was easy to find children with genetic disabilities who were in medical distress because they spent a lot of time in the hospital. The danger of using these children for experiential learning was that they gave a skewed sense that disability and disease are one and the same. There are many genetic disabilities—Down syndrome among them—that often have relatively little impact on a person's quality of life. People with Down syndrome aren't sick; they are disabled. But healthy children with disabilities are harder to track down. That's why Colleen and I were such a goldmine. We were eager to talk, and had connections to a large and diverse network of families who might be willing to do the same.

I came away from these meetings pleasantly surprised. I appreciated discovering that this new generation of genetic counselors in training was skeptical about the purpose and value of the race for genetic knowledge. They didn't see it as their job to perpetuate more and more genetic testing, but rather to help people sort through the overwhelming abundance of available genetic information.

I also loved the feeling of speaking as a parent. As a scholar, I spent a lot of time doubting my own conclusions, wondering whether the evidence I had collected really supported the arguments I wanted to make and why anyone should care. The more I learned the less I seemed to know. No matter how thorough my research, I always felt like I should have read more, thought more deeply, spent more time in the archives. This time, the archive consisted of my own experiences and the knowledge they had brought me. Professors in the humanities have been skeptical of personal experience as a source of evidence. We say that people are unreliable narrators, no better at representing their own feelings and experiences than anyone else. True enough. Still, this was a situation where personal experience made me an authority simply because it was mine. It wasn't the kind of authority I enjoyed as a tenured professor. I wasn't claiming to speak for other people, or to know everything. I was just talking about the things that had happened to me to an audience that believed those things were worth listening to. It felt simple and genuine, and I found it very gratifying.

At the same time, I couldn't help questioning whether we would make much of a difference. I was struck by the youth and relative sameness of the genetic counseling students. There were at least fifty people in the room, and only one of them was male. Almost everyone was white. In their sweatshirts and ponytails, they looked a lot like Sarah Lawrence undergraduates. I didn't doubt their sincerity, but I wondered how effective those students would be when they left the best genetic counseling program in the country to confront the staggering diversity of the families who need their services. I wondered, given their age and inexperience, how seriously they would be taken by expectant parents. And I was skeptical about whether they would be heard by doctors and researchers in a professional environment where genetic counselors are at the bottom of the pecking order.

I predict that some of those women will eventually conclude that their guidance comes at the wrong time. At the point when most people meet a genetic counselor, they're already in a situation of too little, too late. Counselors ask prospective parents to think about what it means to have a child, what kinds of lives are to be valued and wanted, and what resources and opportunities are available to people born with genetic disabilities and their families. Surely there's a better time and place for those conversations. These questions about family, parenting, and disability should be widely debated by our society as a whole so that pregnant women come to the crossroads of prenatal testing better prepared for the choices they need to make. Of course, the ultimate decisions will always have to lie with individual families, particularly with the pregnant woman. Henry hadn't shaken my belief that all women have the right to reproductive freedom, whether that means abortion or choosing to bear a disabled fetus. In fact, he had strengthened my sense of conviction. No woman should be forced to give birth to an unwanted child. But the information about prenatal testing is so often riddled with bias and inaccuracies that foreclose the possibility of making thoughtful and genuine decisions. Expectant parents might make different choices if there were better information and more public debate about the meaning and purpose of the knowledge genetic science makes available to us. These debates are tremendously important, given how many expectant parents now confront decisions about genetics in some form or another. No matter how well intentioned the genetic counselors may be, I'm not sure that they are adequately equipped to mediate the competing interests of expectant parents, clinicians, and scientists.

OUR SECOND SET OF MEETINGS took us into the belly of the beast. We were invited back to the hospital where Aaron was born, this time to speak to a group of obstetrical residents. Our presentation was scheduled to take place in a conference room on the very floor where babies where delivered. Colleen and I waited for our host, Lucy

Nelson, in the same room where pregnant women were being admitted to give birth. Along the hall, open doors revealed women in various stages of labor.

Truth be told, I was more intrigued to meet the obstetricians than I was to meet the genetic counselors. The obstetrical residents excited me. They're the ones on the front lines, who first broach the subject of genetic testing, deliver the news about genes gone awry, and have the first opportunity to manage the expectant parents' response. This was my chance to make up for that moment when the resident who delivered my baby sewed me up and vanished out of my life. If I couldn't talk back to him, at least I could tell my story to this new group of residents. Maybe they would think twice about running away if they ever found themselves in his situation.

The glitch I saw in the system of obstetrical training was that the very doctors who devote themselves to helping women achieve a healthy pregnancy often know nothing at all about children. This division of labor seems to work fine for a typical baby. A woman gives birth under the obstetrician's care, and the infant is immediately handed over to a pediatrician. But long before that, the obstetrician is also required to help expectant parents make sense of genetic information about the fetus. How can an obstetrician be expected to manage the news that a fetus has Down syndrome or Kleinfelter's or spina bifida when she's ignorant about what it's like to live with, or parent a child with, those conditions? I remembered Dr. Lewis's feeble attempt to comfort me by saying that a girl with Down syndrome lived in her neighborhood. At the time I wondered bitterly whether that was really the best she could do after all her years of medical training?

The fact of the matter is that, unlike the best genetic counseling programs, an obstetrical residency doesn't involve exposure to people with genetic disabilities. Many obstetricians agree that this is a problem. In a 2004 survey of medical students, the majority reported that they had received no clinical training about people with intellectual disabilities. Among the American Congress of Obstetricians and Gynecologists fellows questioned the same year, 45 percent claimed that their preparation to deliver a prenatal diagnosis was "barely adequate or non-existent." I went to the hospital with these statistics in mind, convinced that I had something important to teach these residents, but also knowing they might not appreciate what I had to say.

Lucy Nelson, a genetic counselor who coordinated lectures for the obstetrical residents, greeted us warmly and led us to the conference room where we would speak. It was a cluttered, windowless space. On the back wall, screens blinked and hummed, displaying the vital signs of the women in labor down the hall. Our audience was dressed in scrubs, beepers at hand. I was again struck by their youth.

An earlier presentation was running overtime, and we were asked to wait at the back of the room. The speaker, who I later learned was the hospital's chairman of obstetrics and gynecology, was just finishing. I watched him read his Blackberry as he talked. Then he started to type. "Any questions?" he asked, without looking up. There were none. He collected his belongings and left. The residents stayed seated for our presentation.

I let Colleen speak first. She described being devastated by the prenatal diagnosis of Down syndrome, what it felt like to break the news to friends and family, and the strain of having to repeatedly justify her decision to keep the pregnancy. Some doctors she consulted seemed to assume she would have an abortion. Others offered useless insight, like the cardiologist who told her husband that their son would probably never write the great American novel. "Neither will I," he responded. Colleen said how much it meant to her when a doctor congratulated her on the birth of her son, as she imagined he would have done with any other baby. She told the residents how important it was not to assume that parents would see a baby with Down syndrome as a tragedy.

At this point, a youngish resident broke in. "Excuse me, but I need to make a comment. You're telling us what to say and how to act. But I don't think you understand. In a situation like this, we're dealing with the shock of the birth too." His voice rose. "Before you had your son, did you ever know someone who was pregnant with a baby with Down syndrome? Well, neither did any of us. We don't see this every day. How do you think we feel? We have feelings, just like other people."

Colleen bristled.

Another resident jumped in to chide her colleague. She told him that his feelings shouldn't matter. They shouldn't influence his treatment of new parents in need of his compassion and medical expertise. Others chimed in, and for a minute everybody was talking at once.

He sat back, chagrined but still agitated.

The discussion turned to how parents' cultural backgrounds might influence their response to the news that their new baby had a genetic disorder. By that point, our presentation had been completely derailed. Our hour was almost over and I had only a few minutes to summarize what I had planned to say.

Afterward, Lucy apologized for the student's outburst. "I'm sorry we ran out of time before you got to tell your story," she said.

I didn't mind. Much as I had looked forward to having the tables turned so that I got to speak while the doctors listened, I knew I had learned something important. What I heard the agitated resident telling us was that his training—focused intently as it was on curing and preventing illness—gave him no mechanism for attending to his patients' shock, pain, and grief. Or to the emotional baggage he took away after encountering their suffering. I realized he wasn't ready to hear my story. How could he accept what Colleen and I had to say when he so clearly felt that his own needs had not been attended to? I found myself in the strange position of empathizing with someone who seemed very much like the resident who had cut and run from the scene of Henry's birth.

I asked Lucy whether I could come back, not to finish the presentation as I had planned, but to lead a guided reading and writing exercise about delivering and receiving shattering news. I thought that maybe if I could shift the focus onto the residents and their experiences, we would better understand each other, and that understanding could become the basis for real dialogue.

When I went back for our second visit, it was less as a parent than as a professor, prepared with some strategies borrowed from friends in the Narrative Medicine Program at Columbia. Practitioners of narrative medicine believe that doctors and patients need more opportunities to tell their stories. They assume that doctors who make the effort to work through their own pain and anxiety become better listeners and interpreters of their patients' experiences. Using literature as a guide, they help students to understand how narrative is constructed. Literary texts become a basis for creating and analyzing narratives of their own, which should provide them with the strength and wisdom to interpret the narratives presented by their patients.

I asked the residents at the hospital to read a passage from a short story about a baby diagnosed with renal cancer. I had them write for five minutes, reflecting on how the author describes the relationship between doctor and patients. We had a brief discussion about what they had written. My own interpretation focused on how the parents were disempowered by the layout of the room and the way the doctor approached them. The residents countered by noting the absence of the doctor's point of view. Then I asked them to use what they had gathered from the passage to write about their own experience of breaking difficult news.

After a few minutes, I asked them to share their responses. The man who had responded so vehemently to Colleen's story wrote about standing outside the room of a woman who had just been diagnosed with terminal cancer, trying to work up the nerve to approach her as she lay in bed surrounded by her family. The resident sitting next to him wrote about helping to deliver a baby that was sure to die within hours of birth. Another wrote about having to tell someone her fetus was already dead. I asked whether they had ever been invited to share these stories before. They shook their heads. I looked around the room, noticing again how young they were and thinking about what it would be like to confront suffering and death on a daily basis. Suddenly, one of the monitors on the wall started to beep loudly. Pagers began to go off. "That's us," someone said. "We've got to go!" They scooped up their charts and stethoscopes and, before we knew it, the room was empty.

To thank us, Lucy took Colleen and me to lunch. She was sorry our session had ended so abruptly and said she thought the exercise had been valuable for the residents. I told her it had been valuable for me as well. From the interaction I had witnessed between the residents and the department chairman before our first meeting, I could see that they needed someone to listen to them just as much as they needed to learn how to better listen to their patients.

She agreed that the chairman was a terrible listener. She and her colleagues had seen him write on his Blackberry while talking to patients as well as to residents. "But that was also a terrible day," she said. "We had just got news that the hospital might be closing, and he was talking to them about applying to other hospitals where they could continue their residencies. Everybody was under so much stress. Things are much better now. They've decided to let things stand for the time being."

I said I was glad. I appreciated the residents' honesty and their willingness to participate in an exercise that must have seemed alien to them. The medical system that was training them left so little time for dialogue between doctors and patients, let alone opportunities for doctors to reflect on the meaning of what their patients were saying. In asking these residents to be sensitive about Down syndrome, we were getting ahead of ourselves. First they had to learn to see their patients' personhood, to remember that beyond their isolated symptoms and complaints, they were human beings with complex needs and desires. And to get there, they needed to confront their own feelings about the difficult and sometimes tragic nature of their work. Most doctors go into medicine out of a genuine desire to help. Somewhere along the way, their training, the hierarchies of their profession, and the bureaucratic mess of our health care system conspire to make many of them forget. I found it gratifying to think that my training as a teacher of literature might help them to remember why they were there. Lucy and I talked about planning some future sessions, maybe even starting an ongoing reading and writing group. A week later, I read in the newspaper that the hospital would close for good and that the entire staff would lose their jobs.

Cake

JON AND I DON'T LIVE in the kind of world where people say that Henry was sent to us for a reason. My mother-in-law, HuEllen, does. In late summer she started planning our holiday visit to Georgia. We would travel there a few days before Christmas and stay through her birthday on December 27. She called every few days to let us know how excited she was. She, and all the people she ran into at the local Kroger, the mall, and church, who just couldn't wait to meet Henry. She was planning to throw him a big birthday party, where she could introduce him to her friends and family. It meant a lot to me that HuEllen had been madly in love with Henry ever since that first day she held him in the NICU. She continued to treat him as if he were just as smart and capable as her other grandchildren. In fact, neither side of our family seemed to have any trouble appreciating Henry. Still, most of the appreciation had happened at a distance, or during visits on our own turf. This was the first time we would travel with Henry to an entirely new setting, one where I had never felt fully comfortable myself.

In my in-laws' world, I was pretty sure there were still people who understood disabilities as signs from God. Sometimes they were seen as signals of a person's special forbearance or goodness. And sometimes they were lessons in some charitable virtue like patience, acceptance, or humility. I had read plenty of websites, blogs, and memoirs whose authors claimed people with Down syndrome were angels, or that God had singled out their families for the special mission of raising a child with a disability. I could accept that there are many different ways to make sense of disability, but this one seemed both grandiose and misguided. To call someone an angel is to risk losing sight of the complexities that make him the person he is, only some of which have to do with Down syndrome. I didn't know what I would do if someone spoke to me about Henry in that way.

When the day of our trip finally rolled around, Henry had a bad cold. Despite my careful planning, the morning of our departure was chaotic. We raced around the apartment trying to get everyone dressed, taking out the garbage, and stuffing last-minute additions into our suitcases. We could tell Henry felt awful. He was usually cheery and easygoing, but that morning he was cranky and refused to let us put him down. His eyes were wet and swollen, and no matter how often we wiped his runny nose, he scrubbed at it until his face was slick with snot. During the flight he lay draped over Jon's shoulder, half asleep in pool of drool and mucus. Every so often he would raise his head to cry weakly, then slump back down with exhaustion.

Things didn't improve when we got to Georgia. Henry was miserable for much of the visit. His nose continued to run and he had a fever. Normally, he loved new places and people, but his sickness made him anxious and grumpy. After waiting for months to cuddle with her youngest grandson, HuEllen was rebuffed. Henry didn't want to be held by anyone except me or Jon, and he cried and fussed whenever I tried to leave the room.

Cake

On the night before the party, I made Henry's birthday cake. Call me crazy, but one of the reasons I wanted children was so that I could bake them birthday cakes. I love cake. I love its frivolity and decadence. I love the drawn-out process of baking and cooling, filling, and icing. I love the way a frosted cake sits there like a blank canvas, full of potential as it waits to be decked out with its final embellishments. I love the moment after the first cut, when I draw out a slice that reveals the contrasts of color and texture inside. I love the way cake tastes, the sweet dry crumb moistened by the frosting's cool smoothness. My cakes are always meant for an audience, and while I bake and decorate I imagine other people eating them. I love the fact that cake has no other purpose than to make people happy, to lend sweetness and color to a festive moment. Best of all, I love the leftover piece of cake to be eaten—maybe with the last of the ice cream—in the quiet after the party is over and the dishes washed and put away.

I decided to make Henry a white almond cake, since Noah didn't like chocolate. Because I never use a timer, my baking relies a lot on smell and sight. Before checking on a baking cake, you need to make sure it's firm enough to withstand the colder air that comes in when the oven door is opened. I have good instincts and hardly ever make a mistake, but I hadn't used HuEllen's oven before. This cake fell when I tried to see if it was done, the center collapsing into a soggy wrinkled crater. HuEllen clucked with disappointment, but I thought it could be saved. Once I spread the layers with vanilla custard and frosted it with whipped cream, the damage was hardly noticeable. I decorated the top with clowns and balloons, and knew that nobody would notice if the cake was a bit dense in the middle.

By the morning of the party, Henry was feeling better and he seemed to be adjusting to the new space. He let HuEllen hold him and

Cake

played happily with his rubber giraffe. Still, I could feel myself getting tense as the guests started to arrive. The front hall echoed with cheery cries of "hey y'all." I found myself clasped in energetic hugs, my head pressed against warm, perfumy holiday sweaters and freshly washed hair. Henry smiled at the commotion, pushing a ball around the living room rug. The guests cooed appreciatively, and he cooed back, delighted by the attention.

One of Jon's cousins came in with his wife and daughter, who was just a week younger than Henry. They plopped her on the rug and I watched her walk unsteadily around the coffee table, holding it for support while sweeping everything in her path to the floor. For a moment, I thought about the likelihood that it would be another year before Henry could walk. Then I reminded myself how good it was to know that he would walk, even if he took his own sweet time to do it. Surprisingly, I sort of believed it. I realized that at least an hour had gone by and nobody had mentioned God or angels or Jesus. Nobody had described Henry as a gift or a blessing. In fact, nobody seemed to regard him as anything other than the baby that he was.

And then it was time for the cake. After the candle and the singing and the cutting, we sat Henry in a highchair with a slice on his tray. HuEllen had her heart set on a cake shot, but I doubted he would want to try it. We were still struggling to get Henry to feed himself, and he tended to resist new textures. When confronted with an unfamiliar food, he usually screwed up his face in disgust and pushed it right back out of his mouth. All of this was made worse by his cold, and he had hardly eaten any solid foods all week. As grandma stood by with the camera, I touched a dab of whipped cream to his lip. He licked it appreciatively. I tried a morsel of cake. He rolled it around in his mouth, his tongue working awkwardly. Then he reached his hand out tentatively, patting the mound of cake in front of him. Hooking his fingers, he raked a big piece into his fist, and raised it to his face. As he chewed, he gazed up at me with a look of solemn delight, as if marveling at how sweet and good the food of the big people could be. I gazed back at him in agreement.

Brothers

NOAH FIRST MET HIS BROTHER when Henry was two days old. We knew it would be a short visit since the NICU was an unwelcoming place for a child who was less than two years old himself. Alarming temptations were everywhere, from the wheeled carts stacked with equipment and supplies to outlets bristling with electrical cords, machines that blinked and hummed, and switches and buttons crying out to be pressed, not to mention the tiny, fragile babies struggling for life in their plastic bubbles.

I had low expectations for this meeting. Unlike some of the girls at preschool, Noah showed absolutely no interest in babies. Although he played happily in the miniature kitchen in the Toddler Room, he ignored the doll-sized highchairs, cribs, and strollers, and would step mercilessly on the baby dolls that happened to be left in his path. When the teachers brought real babies to visit from the room next door, he looked right through them. Before Henry was born, I had bought Noah a stack of books about being a big brother. He liked them well enough, but showed no sign that he understood, much less looked forward to, the prospect of becoming a big brother himself.

Of course, none of those books prepares you to meet a baby who is medically fragile. Sometimes the new baby is brought home by his parents, or sometimes big brother goes to visit his mom in the hospital. But never the NICU, with its cold bright lights and the sounds of machinery keeping its tiny charges alive. As we rode the elevator with Noah, I felt a pang of regret as I realized how far we were from the meeting I had imagined in the months leading up to Henry's birth.

Jon held Noah tightly as he navigated the busy floor to get to Henry's pod. Although they had yet to find anything wrong with Henry, the doctors continued to treat him like he was gravely ill. We found him lying in his crib, alert and looking out at his surroundings as his legs kicked busily in a tangle of blanket and wires. Jon held Noah at eye level so he could peer inside. "This is your brother Henry," I said.

Noah looked curiously at the baby on the other side of the plastic shield. We waited expectantly for some response. For a second, I thought he might be losing interest. But then he cried out, "He's wearing diapers too!"

"Why yes, he is," Jon answered, and we all burst out laughing. Here was a first sign of brotherly recognition. It wasn't the sensors, the wires, the feeding tube or the monitors that attracted Noah. Instead, it was the amazing discovery that this strange baby wore diapers, just like he did.

From that first meeting, I should have known how rarely my expectations for Noah as a big brother would align with reality. There were some pleasant surprises, but also unexpected difficulties. Introducing a second child into a family is never easy, and the challenges are magnified when that child is born with a disability. Henry demanded a much different kind of attention than Noah had when he was a baby. We couldn't just park him quietly in a corner and wait for him to grow up, as was the usual fate of the younger sibling. In Henry's first weeks at home, not only did Rosalyn take up residence in our living room, but there were several appointments with a visiting nurse service, and repeat sessions with a lactation consultant. There were the usual trips to the pediatrician, but also half-day marathons with a cardiologist, gastrointestinal specialist, and urologist. I was constantly on the phone. Numerous appointments had to be made to get Henry evaluated for early intervention services. Although he had no apparent medical problems, I worried constantly about his feeding, his muscle weakness, his heart, and his enlarged kidney. After those concerns were mostly put to rest, my worries shifted to his development: Was he getting enough stimulation? Was he being overstimulated? Was he positioned in a way that would give his muscles optimal input? Was he getting enough rest? Was he sleeping too much? Did his day have enough structure? Was his schedule too rigid? It was impossible for me to relax and just let Henry be. I felt no confidence that his body or mind would know what to do to ensure proper development. Whatever I was doing with Noah, I was always aware that I might be doing something more for Henry, something that might make a difference for his future.

Noah had a personality that simply wouldn't accept playing second fiddle to a younger brother, no matter what the circumstances. The books on growing up with a disabled child in the family report that the able-bodied child is often neglected, his needs subordinated to the more pressing demands of the sibling with a disability. This can lead to all sorts of consequences, from hostility and resentment to perfectionism and overachievement as compensation for the sibling who is perceived to be lacking. That was never the dynamic in our family. It was partly that Noah was good at putting himself in the spotlight, something Jon and I allowed and even encouraged. Each of us was the elder of two children and knew what it was like to endure a younger sibling who was always cuter, needier, and more demanding than we were. When my sister was born, I was too young to remember life as a singleton, but Jon, who was four at the time, could clearly recall the day his brother came home from the hospital. We were sensitive, perhaps excessively so, to the disruption Henry introduced into Noah's world.

It was also true that Henry was an exceptionally easygoing and contented baby. He was surprisingly healthy, given the many concerns the doctors raised around his birth. His worst complaint was a runny nose that lasted from October to May, thanks to the numerous viruses Noah brought home from preschool. And much as I worried about the developmental consequences of leaving Henry on the sidelines, he was perfectly happy to watch his big brother Noah being the center of attention. In my less anxious moods, I could see the real benefits of having an older sibling to serve as a model.

In the beginning, I tried to be everything to everybody. I would cook a meal, putting Henry to sleep strapped to my chest in his baby carrier (an explicit no-no, according to the instructions on the box) while playing a game with Noah. I would do Henry's therapy exercises while feeding dinner to Noah and planning the next day's errands in my head. I would read Noah a book while dangling a ring in front of Henry's eyes to stimulate his tracking skills. One night, Noah dropped a toy behind the couch while I was nursing Henry. Unable to reach it, he began to demand, with growing urgency escalating toward a tantrum, that I get it for him. I should have told him firmly to wait until I was finished. But the memory of being rejected was still fresh, and I was irrationally eager to please. So I dropped to my knees, clutching Henry to my bare breast with one arm while fumbling under the couch with the other. As I groped blindly beneath the furniture, my sleeve caught in an old glue trap put out some months ago to catch a mouse that had been spotted in our living room. After badly wrenching my neck, I finally managed to get my hands on the toy and emerged, dripping with sweat, the trap dangling from my shirt as Henry continued to nurse contentedly. I realized that there was no way to get the trap unglued from my shirt without disturbing Henry, so I peeled off everything except the sleeve closest to the arm that was supporting him. Wearing only my bra and old sweatpants, I handed the toy back to Noah and burst into the kind of laughter that could easily become tears.

When incidents like this happened, I realized how much my attention was constantly scattered. I felt exhausted by trying to do too many things at once, making sure that nobody was left out or over-looked. Even worse was when we tried to divide and conquer, Jon taking one child and leaving me with the other. Since Henry's birth, whenever Noah had his choice of parents, he wanted Jon. I knew perfectly well that his two-year-old mind wasn't rational. I knew this was his way of asserting control over an uncertain world. And I knew it probably wouldn't last forever. Still, it drove me wild with jealousy. In some deep, unacknowledged way, I felt that Noah was my whole and perfect child. No sooner had he emerged out of babyhood to become a conscious being than he wanted to escape me. Whenever I forced myself on Noah, he whined for daddy. When I gave in and took Henry, I envied the time that Jon and Noah were spending alone together. It was during this difficult time that Peggy, who had been such an incredible source of strength and support just after Henry's birth, gave me her worst, if most memorable, advice. I went to her in desperation to ask how to regain Noah's trust. She shrugged. "Kids have preferences," she said matter-of-factly. "Sometimes they kick in early. It may be that he just prefers his dad."

I cried all the way home, imagining a lifetime in which I was the third wheel to the warm, intimate relationship Jon would share with Noah.

I knew the primary reason for Noah's rejection was that he held me responsible for bringing Henry into the world. First I had grown fat and tired with pregnancy, and then, even worse, I had forced an unwanted baby brother into his life. Noah was punishing me for not being there, for not making him the exclusive object of my attention. Yet in spite of the unyielding cold shoulder he turned to me, Noah never once took his resentment out on Henry. Before Henry was born, more than one person had warned us not to leave him alone with Noah. We had heard stories about older siblings who tried to harm a new baby. Even Jon's parents didn't think it was safe to let them share a room. But Noah was never rough, and his hostility was never directed at Henry. Instead he treated his brother with a studied indifference, as if he hoped that ignoring the new baby might just make him go away.

Of course, things didn't go on like this forever, although it seemed like it at the time. Almost exactly a year after Henry was born, Noah began to realize he didn't have to constantly play one parent off the other. He seemed to forgive me for bringing a strange baby into our lives, or perhaps he just forgot he'd ever had a life without Henry. Whatever the reason, Noah started wanting to spend time with both parents. Sometimes he even showed a preference for me, but mostly he began to want the whole family to be together. Even better, he started to enjoy his brother. Henry had reached an age where he could respond to Noah, the most brilliant and entertaining person he had ever met. When Noah made funny faces or loud noises, Henry would scream with delight. Noah discovered that he could egg Henry on, encouraging him to do forbidden things like blowing raspberries with food in his mouth or jumping on the couch. Much as we wished Henry wouldn't do these things, we also loved seeing our sons taking such evident pleasure in each other's company.

As Henry started to move around, wrestling became his favorite way of interacting with Noah. Along with his low muscle tone, Henry had decreased sensory awareness, which meant that he enjoyed rough play of all kinds. He loved the feeling of being vigorously pushed, thrown, bounced, and jostled. When Noah eventually got tired, Henry would continue to throw himself from one end of the couch to the other, crying out with joy as he hit the cushions and got up for more. Sometimes when Noah declared the game over, Henry refused to leave him alone. It took a while for him to calm down after being engaged in such tussles. Wild with excitement, he would poke Noah in the eyes, pull his hair, or throw himself at Noah's back, laughing uproariously even while Noah cried out in protest. But no matter how annoying these unwanted advances, Noah was always gentle. Although he was far bigger and heavier, he knew how to restrain himself while Henry, caught up in the frenzy of the moment, lost all sense of how rough he was being.

After so many months of trying to do and be everything, I loved just sitting back and watching my sons play together. I didn't mind if they screamed or jumped on the furniture or threw our once-stylish sofa cushions to the floor because I was so happy they were enjoying each other. Even when laughter turned to tears, the injuries were quickly forgotten. I knew I was seeing the beginning of a relationship that had nothing to do with Down syndrome, or disability of any kind.

And that was exactly how we wanted it. Jon and I had very deliberately chosen not to tell Noah that Henry had Down syndrome. Better to let him know his brother as a person, we reasoned. There would be time enough for him to learn about Down syndrome and the challenges his brother might face as he grew up and went out into the world. There would be sad lessons about the intolerance and ignorance of others. And inevitably, there would be periods when Noah felt ashamed and burdened by his brother's disability. Given the difficulties that waited on the horizon, we felt no need to force Noah to an early realization of the ways his brother might be different from other people.

It wasn't that we kept Down syndrome a secret, exactly. We talked about it openly in Noah's presence, and brought him to events like the Down Syndrome Buddy Walk and play dates organized by our parents group. I also bought him books like *I Can, Can You?* and *Hi, I'm Ben and I've Got a Secret*, which featured children with Down syndrome. Our favorite was *Be Quiet Marina!* about the friendship between a girl with Down syndrome and a girl with cerebral palsy. I liked the book because it didn't mention the girls' disabilities, focusing on their relationship rather than their differences from other children. Noah liked it because Marina made a lot of noise, and reading it properly required vigorous shouting. He enjoyed all of these books, but showed no sign that he thought they had anything to do with him or our family. We saw no reason to tell him otherwise. Why label Henry at such a young age, before we really knew who he was or what he was capable of becoming?

Still, I worried constantly about what it would mean for Noah to grow up with a disabled brother. My godmother, Diane, had a son with an intellectual disability. Josh had a remarkable memory and could be hilariously funny, but he also had a violent temper. Once, in a fit of rage, he kicked a car so hard that he left a dent. Sometimes, he attacked his sister Naomi. One day he punched her in the face while she was having her temperature taken, shattering the thermometer to pieces in her mouth. Another time, after a day of sailing, he wrestled her to the dock while Diane looked on, terrified that they would both roll off into the ocean. As an adult, Josh lived in a group home where his behavior was controlled by medication. His doctors never seemed to get the dosage right and he was often in a semicatatonic state during holiday visits, unable to make conversation or even remember who we were. I knew that growing up with Josh had left its mark on Naomi. She had an intuitive understanding of people with intellectual disabilities, and spent several years working at the boarding school where Josh had been a student. But she also spoke of her resentment at being sidelined by her brother's tantrums. She hated the way her mother caved in to Josh's requests for food and presents, their visits centering around his demands. Despite having worked with disabled people, she still cringed in disgust at Josh's loud, greedy behavior at mealtimes. I often wondered whether Naomi's insistence that she never wanted children came from seeing her mother struggle to raise Josh.

Of course I knew Henry wasn't Josh, and that he was unlikely to share Josh's personality or difficult behaviors. But I also knew he would present Noah with challenges that his friends with nondisabled siblings wouldn't have to face. I had done enough reading to know that Naomi's experiences were fairly typical. Siblings of children with disabilities often complain of feeling isolated and confused. When they are young, they may worry about contracting the sibling's disability, or be stricken by a sense of guilt that they are responsible for causing it. They may worry deeply about the disabled sibling's health and well-being. They may feel compelled to be perfect in order to compensate for the obvious imperfections of the disabled sibling. They may also act out, resenting the attention that goes into caring for the disabled sibling. At some point, the typical child becomes aware that the sibling is perceived differently by others, and may feel shame, embarrassment, and rejection. As time passes, nondisabled siblings often fear they will be responsible for the long-term care of a disabled brother or sister. Of course, the news wasn't all bad. It seemed that growing up with a disabled sibling could also infuse a person with a greater sense of responsibility, patience, and compassion for others. Some siblings are inspired to go into helping professions, such as medicine, teaching, or public interest law. Others translate their early experience with disability into a greater appreciation for, and understanding of, the wide spectrum of human differences.

With all this in mind, I signed up for a conference sponsored by YAI, the organization that provided Henry's early intervention services. I noticed there were several panels on sibling relationships, and thought I could learn something from hearing what the presenters had to say. The most meaningful session featured four pairs of brothers and sisters. Each pair was made up of one disabled and one typical sibling in conversation about what it was like to grow up together. Some of what they said was familiar, but I found it much more powerful to hear it than to read it in a book. I was struck by the warmth and ease of their relationships, and by the patient and respectful behavior of the nondisabled siblings, but also by the fact that these brothers and sisters shared the same kinds of memories, inside jokes, and gentle bickering that is a part of so many utterly typical families. It was also important for me to hear their individual stories. A youngish man described himself as a failure at school and work. Unmotivated by his studies and with few career plans, he began to coach his sister's Special Olympics team, finding a sense of purpose and joy in working with them. Once he realized how much he liked spending time with his sister, he proposed that they start a document destruction business together. They bought a truck and a shredding machine. Her autistic temperament gave her prodigious powers of concentration, allowing her to sit contentedly in the back of the truck, shredding paper for many hours at a time while he took care of the business end of things. Another woman took evident pleasure in her disabled brother's company. Laughing and interrupting each other, they told stories about the funny things that happened when he came to visit her. She explained that she and her fiancé were making arrangements for her brother to live nearby. A third woman had very little verbal ability. Her sister carefully explained the efforts the family was making to help her express her desires and plan for her future.

I felt moved and heartened by what I heard. But even as I listened, I was distracted by nagging questions: When did the panelists first learn about their siblings' disability? How was it described to them? What did they think about it? Did they have more disturbing stories that just weren't being shared?

When the presentations ended, there was time for discussion. I struggled to get up the nerve to ask my questions. I was used to asking questions at academic panels, but here I felt shy and awkward. Finally I forced myself to raise a hand. I told them my older son was three, and that his baby brother had Down syndrome. "We haven't told him," I said. "We want him to know his brother as a person, not a diagnosis."

Immediately, as if speaking in one voice, the panelists replied, "You have to tell him right away!" Tell him only things he was capable of understanding, they added, but it was essential for the issue of disability to be out in the open. They insisted that, despite his age, it was very likely Noah had already picked up on the fact that Henry was different. In the absence of any explanation, with time he would invent his own stories about how and why. He might imagine that he was to blame for Henry's disability or fear that someday he too would become disabled. He might resent us for withholding information.

When the panel was over, a woman sitting behind me introduced herself. Her younger brother had Down syndrome, and her parents had never told this to either child. To this day, he continued to ask why he couldn't drive a car or go to law school. As a child, she had imagined terrible things. Praised for her beauty and intelligence, she grew up believing she had greedily stolen these qualities from her brother. She also told me that her brother was funny and charming. He liked to paint and sing, and was a cherished member of the family. She was a philosophy professor at a nearby university, and had focused her work on incorporating intellectual disability into conceptions of family, citizenship, and justice.

Immediately after the panel, I called Jon and said I thought we needed to tell Noah right away. He agreed, although he insisted we had to find the right moment. "Maybe at night just before he goes to sleep. When we're talking over his day," he said.

That night, I was filled with apprehension as I waited for our bedtime conversation. Once Noah was comfortably installed in bed, I began. "Sweetie, do you know what Down syndrome is?" I asked hesitantly.

He shook his head no.

"Does someone in our family have Down syndrome?" I asked.

He nodded, "My brother Henry."

"Do you want to know what that means?" Jon asked.

"Okay."

"It means he'll be a little bit slower to do some things. Like walking and talking. That's why he has so many therapists, to help him. He'll do all the same things as other kids, but it will be more challenging for him, and it will take him longer."

"Okay."

"We want you to know that if you have any questions, ever, about Down syndrome, you can always ask. This is something you can talk about with us."

"Okay."

We waited for some further acknowledgment. Noah turned over to face us. "Um . . . can we go to the park tomorrow?"

That was the end of our conversation. Occasionally Noah asked a question. Once he told me he could recognize people with Down syndrome, that they looked "like Henry." But by and large, Henry was just Henry, a part of the fabric of our family life like any other brother.

Some time later, Henry's friend Caleb, who also has Down syndrome, was spending the day with us. We took all three boys to visit another family. When we arrived at the apartment, their two boys ran up to meet the elevator. As I unloaded Caleb from the stroller, the older son asked, "Is he Noah's brother?"

"No, silly!" I said. "Noah's brother is Henry, remember?" Then I was curious. "Why did you think Caleb was Noah's brother?"

"Because they look alike, silly!" he cried.

I looked at Caleb. I didn't see much resemblance, aside from the fact that he had straight brown hair, like Noah. But then again, Henry and Noah didn't look much alike either. What pleased me was that this boy hadn't suggested that he saw any resemblance between Henry and Caleb. At age five, Down syndrome was still illegible to him. He knew nothing of features that, for some people, would be the unmistakable signs of stigma, regardless of what our children accomplished in the world. I knew this innocence wouldn't last. Soon enough he would become adept at reading the markers of disability, just as he would those of race. As the child of a white mother and a black father, he too was likely to struggle with the assumptions other people would make about his physical appearance. But for that day, I enjoyed the thought that he could mistake Caleb and Noah for brothers as I watched these five boys of different colors and abilities make their way, shrieking and laughing, into the apartment.

Inclusion

BY THE TIME HENRY WAS a few months old, I had learned that several children with Down syndrome attended a daycare/preschool less than two blocks from our apartment. From our kitchen window, I could see the red brick walls of the Bank Street Family Center, which offered an integrated program where disabled and nondisabled children attended class together. It had a full staff of therapists, teachers who specialized in inclusive education, and classrooms set up to accommodate children with different abilities and needs. For a child like Henry, who absorbed the doings of his nondisabled peers like an eager sponge, it seemed like it could be a perfect fit.

I knew that the Family Center admitted babies as young as six months because I had toured a few years before, when I was looking at daycare options for Noah. I liked it well enough, although I thought the classrooms were too small for someone of Noah's size and energy. In the end, we didn't even get an interview. The decision was made for us when our application fee was returned with a polite form letter saying they had no space for our child. A neighbor told me that when her daughter was rejected, she managed to wrangle a spot by weeping in the director's office. Crying in front of strangers wasn't my style, so that put an end to Noah's relationship with the Family Center. We were so happy with Basic Trust that we never looked back.

When Peggy said she wanted Henry to go to Basic Trust, we thought the matter was settled. After a year or so at home, he would begin daycare in the Baby and Toddler Rooms, and then graduate to the Big Kids Room for his preschool years. This seemed like an ideal scenario. Our lives would be simplified by having both kids in the same school, and Henry would have exactly the same opportunities as his brother. Instead of being labeled as "the kid with Down syndrome," our son would just be Henry. Maybe a bit slower than the others, but still a part of the group.

As time passed, I came to see that my plan wasn't very realistic. I knew the teachers at Basic Trust would be caring and resourceful. I knew they would accept Henry for who he was. They would treat him just like all the other kids in the room, and I loved them for it. But what I started to realize was that, no matter how good the intention, Basic Trust simply wasn't set up to accommodate Henry's needs. Much as he was a child like other children, he also had cognitive and motor delays that would only become more pronounced as time went on. The delays might not matter when Henry was a baby, but by the time he reached preschool age he would get more out of an environment specially designed for children with many different learning abilities. Early intervention had made me aware of how important it is for a child with Down syndrome to get off to a good start with early and sustained developmental therapy. The more Henry got out of preschool, the better he would be prepared to enter elementary school with his nondisabled classmates.

The Family Center seemed to be exactly what we needed. They were pros at Down syndrome. At the time, four other children with

Down syndrome were enrolled in the program. Three of Henry's early intervention therapists also worked there, which meant that he would know some of the staff. The icing on the cake was that we wouldn't have to pay the hefty tuition. Because the Family Center is classified as a "center-based program," children with disabilities can request a half-day's tuition covered by early intervention. If he were admitted to the Family Center, we could petition to include it along with the other services outlined in Henry's semiannual Individualized Family Service Plan. Attending class in a center-based program is considered an important form of socialization. Early intervention ensures that center-based services are available to the children who need them, even if their families can't afford the cost of tuition. The money that goes into these programs is well spent: giving opportunities to young children with disabilities establishes a foundation that makes it more likely they will be able to function in an inclusive setting in elementary school and beyond.

It's no surprise that the Family Center looked like an oasis, with its welcoming rainbow of races and abilities. The Bank Street School and College of Education had a long history of being at the vanguard of progressive education for both students and teachers in training, serving as a model for other schools in New York and around the country. It began as an experimental nursery school in 1916. Its founder, Lucy Sprague Mitchell, sought to create an educational environment that nurtured all aspects of child development. The Bureau of Educational Experiments, as it was called at the time, also served as a laboratory for teachers and researchers to study how children learn. Drawing on the model of progressive education outlined by the philosopher John Dewey, the Bureau based its curriculum on learning through experience and experimentation. At some point in the 1930s it moved to Bank Street, and the name stuck, despite its relocation to our neighborhood on the Upper West Side.

When Lucy Sprague Mitchell founded her Bureau, it had nothing to do with special education. Until the passage of the 1975 Education for All Handicapped Children Act (EAHCA), the prospects for educating children with disabilities were bleak. Throughout the 1970s and 1980s, children with disabilities continued to receive little educational support until they reached elementary school age. The more I read, the better I understood why earlier generations of parents seemed so ready to institutionalize their children with Down syndrome. The prevailing wisdom was that they were incapable of learning. Best-case scenario, they might someday be taught to feed and dress themselves. And it wasn't just Down syndrome. Many states had laws that barred public schools from educating children with disabilities such as deafness, blindness, and emotional disturbance, as well as other cognitive delays. According to a research study completed in 1970, only one in five children with disabilities had received an education in school.

In this environment, it was a radical move to open a daycare center that welcomed all children, regardless of physical or cognitive ability. The Infant and Family Center was founded in 1974 by members of the Bank Street faculty who wanted their young children to be nearby while they were at work. From the beginning, the center included children with disabilities, although often with more good intentions than expertise.

Teachers struggled over what to do with a deaf boy who was part of the first class of children to attend. Some days he could be smoothly integrated into the group; other days were a constant struggle, and they breathed a sigh of relief when he was picked up. With time, inclusion became a more institutionalized element of the program, which was licensed first by the family court system and then, after the passage of the IDEA, falling under early intervention (for daycare) and the board of education (for preschool-age children). Even as other programs for young children began to open integrated classrooms, the Family Center stood out in its dedication to including more challenging cases of physical and intellectual disability.

I was determined to get a place for Henry at the Family Center. My experience with Noah made me aware that the Darwinian struggle over education in Manhattan begins at a very young age. Every year the *New York Times* runs stories about the extreme measures parents take to get their kids into "feeder preschools" that promise to prepare them for admission to the best college prep schools. It was unlikely that Henry would be taking this path, but the placement process seemed equally brutal for children with disabilities, especially given the limited number of schools available.

I knew I needed to start early. Noah had thrived in the homey, group setting of Basic Trust, and we wanted to give Henry the same. He also had the best chance of getting into the Family Center if admitted to one of the baby rooms, rather than waiting until preschool, when a smaller number of openings were available. I liked the baby rooms at the Family Center because they were "mixed age," including children from six months to two and a half years. If Henry started in September, at nineteen months, he would be in a class with many younger kids. This meant that everyone would be at a different developmental stage: some crawling, others walking; some eating baby food, others taking sandwiches and grapes for lunch; some able to talk, others still babbling; some taking several naps a day, others taking a single long nap after lunch. The room would be set up to accommodate children at all of these stages. In that environment, it would be difficult to tell who was delayed.

I started to lobby Henry's therapists in the hope that they could work some magic with the admissions process. I went to the open house and took the school tour. I filled out our application promptly and carefully, applying my best literary skills to the short essay section. In March, we were invited for a play date. It was a strange experience. Aside from Henry and me, there was only one other mother and child in the room. We were told to let our babies play on the floor, while a team of therapists and teachers sat around and watched them. Nobody said a word, and the room was silent, except for the sounds of our children playing quietly, some creaking chairs and scribbling pens. Later I would learn that this is vintage Bank Street. The idea is to intervene as little as possible, like Dian Fossey and her gorillas. From the early days Bank Street has worked on the belief that educators learn a lot by watching children at play uninhibited by adult guidance. At the time, I found the quiet in the room utterly nerve-wracking. I had no idea what to do with myself. The other mother and I sat awkwardly watching our children, aware that we were being watched. Did they expect me to participate in Henry's play? I wondered. Did I seem uninterested? Was I hovering too much? Should I be friendly to the other mom to show that I would be a good citizen? Or would talking disrupt the observation? After half an hour it was over. The team had seen all it needed to see, and they thanked us for coming. Before I knew it, we were back out in the cold. I didn't know what to think.

READER, HE GOT IN.

In the end I don't think anything I said or did made it happen. The Family Center was looking for kids who might succeed in an inclusion program, and Henry was a good candidate. He was curious, receptive to his environment, and eager to follow the lead of typically developing peers. He was affectionate, alert, and easy to please, showing no signs of behavior that might disrupt the classroom. These qualities, not my well-crafted essays or my efforts to charm the admissions committee, got Henry into the Family Center. Of course, I'd like to believe otherwise. The overachiever in me would like to put this on my shelf alongside other accomplishments like winning the distinguished faculty award and getting Noah into a good elementary school. But there was a more serious undercurrent to my wishful thinking. If I could take credit for getting Henry into daycare, then maybe I could also feel some confidence in my ability to guide him through the far more difficult challenges I saw looming on the horizon. I knew that an inclusive daycare was a walk in the park compared to the kindergarten admissions process for children with disabilities in New York City. Beyond that, I saw many years of struggle to get Henry an education that would allow him to develop to his full potential. But I get ahead of myself.

The Family Center was a wonderful place for Henry, and he quickly grew to love his days there. At first he cried and clung to us when we said goodbye, but soon he was rushing to embrace Gabriel, his "primary," and other teachers in the room. He had an intuitive understanding of how to give affection, reaching out to be handed from parent to teacher, wrapping his chubby arms tightly around Gabriel's neck and nestling his head into her shoulder. Soon he moved on to other activities, the classroom a place of endless entertainment. Henry spent much of his day doing the same things that other children do in daycare. He loved looking at the photocollages of each child's family that the teachers had posted at eye level. He loved climbing onto the lumpy, indestructible couch to survey the activity in the main room. He loved the small back room filled with pretend play activities like dress-up clothes, a miniature kitchen, and doctor's equipment. And he loved crawling up the stairs to the loft, where he could look out the window or read a book. Every day there was a different sensory activity for the kids to explore—a table set up with Play-Doh, foam, bubbles, or various goopy mixtures to rub and squeeze. Henry came home with his clothes and hair covered in paint, glue, glitter, and food. Once a week, a music teacher visited the room. There were art projects, cooking projects, and trips to the park, the farmer's market, neighborhood shops, and the Cathedral of Saint John the Divine to visit the peacocks. Henry also got a lot of therapy, sometimes one-on-one in a special room and other times in his classroom, where other children were included in their activities.

The range of ages in the room made Henry's delays less apparent. He wasn't the only child who didn't yet walk or talk; everybody took naps and wore diapers; some were still eating baby food. Most of the time, we could enjoy the sense that Henry was just an ordinary child, like the others in his class. But then there were moments when I was reminded of his disability, sometimes painfully so. It happened once at the beginning of the year, when Henry first tried to use the sensory table. Piled high with glistening red sand, it caught his eye almost immediately. He scooted over with his lopsided crawl, then laboriously hauled himself to his feet, resting his body weight awkwardly against the edge. He leaned over at a ninety-degree angle, his face just inches from the sand. After eighteen months of early intervention, I had been conditioned to evaluate the merits of every posture. I suspected he wasn't comfortable in that position, and it definitely wasn't good for him. I looked unhappily at the other kids standing upright as they dug and poured. They made it look so easy. An occupational therapist who happened to be in the room saw Henry's difficulties. She quickly came over and repositioned him to make his stance less awkward. Hard as it was to see Henry struggle to do the activities that came easily to his peers, I was comforted to realize that he was surrounded by people who were trained to help.

Another bad moment came on curriculum night. Over the summer, Henry had started to make a lot of noise. We knew this was all for the good, a sign that he had things to say and was strongly motivated to communicate. But so far, the only sound he made with any consistency was an open-mouthed "ah." A typical child who reaches this stage will quickly move on to a babble of other vowels—"oos" and "ees"—and consonants like "ba," "da," and "ma." That Henry was frustratingly stalled at the most basic sounds was all too apparent on curriculum night. The teachers had put together a lovely film showing us what our children did all day. I was pleased to see clips of Henry reading books, playing doctor, and stacking blocks along with his classmates. But the soundtrack made my heart sink. Henry's "ahs" were clearly audible above the sounds of the other children babbling and talking. Even when he wasn't in front of the camera, I could hear his noise in the background, a constant reminder that speech was, and would continue to be, my child's greatest struggle. The rest of the night passed in a blur. Filled with dismay at what I had seen and heard, I could hardly listen to the presentation the teachers had worked so hard to assemble. When it was over, I stumbled out as quickly as I could, avoiding the other parents who were lingering to chat. What did I have to say to these mothers and fathers whose biggest worry was that their kids didn't want to nap or eat green vegetables? I understood where they were coming from, because not so long ago I had been one of them. But now, seeing their children babbling and talking onscreen was a reminder that I had crossed the border into a different world. At that moment I found it hard to imagine any common ground between my situation and theirs.

Inclusion

Curriculum night drove home the more painful side of inclusion. In its truest form, inclusion doesn't mean that everybody can, or will, be expected to do the same things. It's not about dumping children with disabilities into a typical classroom without proper support. At its best, inclusion requires an environment designed to meet the needs of children of many different backgrounds and abilities, and teachers willing to take advantage of the learning opportunities provided by those differences. Time and again, research has shown that everyone benefits from programs that are creative and flexible enough to accommodate disabled and nondisabled students. Kids with disabilities learn a great deal from the modeling of their nondisabled peers, while typical students learn important lessons about the value of human difference. The point isn't just that disabled and nondisabled students can learn from one another. All children learn in different ways, even those who don't have disabilities or Individualized Education Plans. Everybody stands to gain from an inclusive classroom where the curriculum is designed to accommodate varied learning styles and abilities.

Inclusion is also hard work, and it isn't the best option for everyone. In a context where disabled children learn alongside typical peers, their differences become more visible than they might be in an environment where everybody has a diagnosis of one kind or another. As they get older, and the academic and social challenges increase, some kids with disabilities find inclusion stressful and discouraging. Many students who were successfully included in elementary school end up transitioning to more specialized middle and high schools.

It would be years before we had to face this more challenging stage. The wonderful thing about daycare was that none of the kids had any understanding of who was disabled and who wasn't. Unfortunately, the differences were sometimes all too visible to me. I knew that if Henry had gone to a program reserved for children with disabilities, his delays would have been less apparent. I might have felt a greater sense of kinship with other parents who had fought similar battles and faced similar challenges. I might have been spared the realization that other children in the class had reached the stage when they were picking special friends to invite to play dates outside of school. But I also would have missed all the birthday parties where Henry's typical classmates greeted him with hugs, cries of welcome, and invitations to join in their play. And the bonds I formed with other moms and dads around the many joys and struggles of parenting that have nothing to do with ability or disability. Most important, Henry would have missed the opportunity to learn from his typical peers, and to teach them, at a very formative age, the value and importance of diversity that extends beyond gender and skin color.

The differences became more apparent with time. The following year, Henry's December birthday required him to move into the preschool room, along with his older classmates. There, the age range was narrower and his delays more noticeable. Unlike most of his peers, Henry still had impulsive behaviors like eating Play-Doh and throwing toys. By then he could speak a few words, but nothing like the torrent of language I heard from some of his classmates. He loved the other children, and loved being part of a group, but as their games became more elaborate and more dependent on verbal communication, he had trouble knowing how to join in. None of this surprised his teachers, who took it all in stride. Henry was one of five children with disabilities in the class, and I was impressed by how the staff managed to adjust the activities so that everyone could participate. And despite his delays, Henry was growing up, too. He was far more aware of the other children than he had been in Room 1. He loved looking at the pictures of his classmates in the Room 3 Friends book, pointing to each and excitedly crying out their names. He loved going to the library, pretend play, and watching the class pet, a guinea pig named Curly. He impressed his teachers with his physical abilities at the gym and the playground. He was completely fearless and often able to keep up with the older kids. We gave Noah all the credit. Here was the payoff to all the weekend afternoons spent wrestling with Henry, both brothers laughing uproariously until someone got hurt.

I still had my moments: the jolt of sadness when I saw the list of quotes from the students who could talk well enough to describe what it felt like to plant a seed, or my dismay when I learned that Henry had been biting one of the teachers (she generously decided it was her vanilla-scented lotion, and when she stopped using it, the biting stopped too). But mostly I felt grateful that Henry had the opportunity to start his education in a place that gave support in the areas where he was challenged and also allowed him to grow and play alongside typically developing kids. I loved seeing Henry start to make friends. There was one child in particular. She was a small, pretty girl with thick, springy black curls. I found her remarkably mature and articulate for someone just shy of four, and knew that she was capable of engaging with the classroom activities at a very high level. But Henry was her favorite. As soon as she saw him in the morning, she would run over and clench him in a joyful embrace. He was all too happy to return her affection. She would accompany him on his morning trip to the bathroom, where they peed and washed their hands side by side before going into the classroom. There they would read books, draw, or hug some more. One morning after they had kissed repeatedly, she told me soberly that, of course, now they would have to get married some day.

A Simple Place

HENRY WAS THRIVING AT BANK STREET, and during the fall our life started to stabilize into a predictable routine. Both kids were out of the apartment by nine in the morning. Noah spent the full day at Basic Trust, while Henry did a half-day at Bank Street, then came home for a nap and therapy in the afternoon. We had a wonderful nanny named Angela, who was quickly becoming Henry's favorite person in the world. Although everything seemed to be going well, I still felt angry and worried most of the time. Whenever I wasn't dealing with some immediate crisis—and there were still plenty of those—my worries started to spiral out of control. Was I a good mother? Was Henry getting the care he needed? What would his future hold? Finding a French fry in the stroller caused me to lie awake all night worrying that Angela had been taking Henry to McDonald's. Talking to a parent whose child was trying an alternative kind of physical therapy prompted a tailspin of doubt about whether I had made the right choices for Henry. Stumbling over the shoes Jon had left on the floor in the hallway sent me into a fit of rage that he wasn't more helpful in caring for our children.

One night Jon and I watched a DVD of the film *Praying with Lior*, about a boy with Down syndrome who is preparing for his bar mitzvah. It had been recommended by friends, and I looked forward to seeing it. What nobody had mentioned to me was that Lior's mother died when he was six. As much as the film is about the events leading up to Lior's big rite of passage, it's also about how his family managed in the years since her death. I could understand why people loved it. It's impossible not to root for Lior, who is charismatic, funny, and utterly passionate about his religious practice. But watching the film was devastating. One scene includes home movie footage of Lior's mother saying goodbye to her children before she leaves for what would be her final visit to the hospital. She gives each a teddy bear, telling them to hold it when they need her and she can't be there. In another scene, twelve-year-old Lior visits her grave and weeps on his father's shoulder. By that point I was crying so hard I could hardly see the screen. Jon kept asking whether I wanted to turn it off. I shook my head, knowing I needed to finish. But the happy ending didn't make me feel any better. Seeing Lior's loving family, his supportive schoolmates, his joyful bar mitzvah did nothing to lessen my sense of tragedy. His mother wasn't there to share any of it.

When the film was over, Jon tried his best to be comforting. But there wasn't much he could say. I ended up crying myself to sleep. For days afterward, I would burst into tears just thinking about the film. I identified deeply with Lior, who was the same age as I was when my mother died. I knew what it was like to grow up without a mother, each celebration marred by her absence. But I also identified with Lior's mother, and the tragedy of having to leave a child who needed her so much. She puts on a brave face for the camera, but I imagined she was filled with rage at the unfairness of it all. I thought about what it must have been like to realize she wouldn't be there to help her children grow up. I'm sure she felt the loss for each of them, but most of all for Lior.

Praying with Lior made me think differently about why it was so hard for me to trust Angela, and about my feelings of abandonment and doubts about my own performance as a mother. My mother, Ruth, was diagnosed with lung cancer when I was four. The doctors told her that she might live anywhere from three to eighteen months. There was no cure. I have no memories of a time before she was dying, and I grew up aware that life could be cut short at any time. As a child, I studied other children with jealous curiosity. Most of my friends belonged to families that seemed so whole and complete; their happiness seemed to come so easily. I was amazed that anyone could go through life so free of loss. Ruth died when she was forty-two, after an illness that lasted for a year and a half. As I approached that age, I thought a lot about what it would be like for my children to grow up without a mother. We all know we're going to die; awareness of mortality is part of what makes us human. But most people are pretty good at repressing it. The closer I got to forty, the less I was able to shut out the knowledge that someday—maybe fifty years from now, but maybe tomorrow—I would die and leave my children. I realized this fear was behind my desperate need to get things right. It was important to do everything, and to do it perfectly. I wanted to leave my mark on the world, on my children's lives most of all, because I didn't know how long I had. In the middle of ordinary activities like walking in the park with the stroller or sitting at the edge of the sandbox, my imagination would begin to race. I envied the moms and dads chatting on their cell phones or laughing at the funny things their kids were doing as if they didn't have a care in the world. I wondered how it would feel not to think that death and danger lurked around every turn.

Of course, I didn't come to these insights all on my own. Months of crying on my therapist's couch led me to realize that I needed to learn more about my mother. I thought that confronting my fears might help me come to terms with them. During her illness, Ruth kept a journal. I knew that Olivia, the self-appointed family archivist, had it in her closet. I called and asked her to send it to me.

"When I read it, I felt disappointed," she told me. "I thought it would be about what was happening to her. And that there would be more about us. But there isn't much. You'll see."

It turned out there were two books. When they arrived, I understood what she meant. After her diagnosis, Ruth went into Jungian analysis. This wasn't unusual in bohemian southern California of the early 1970s. Analysis shaped her writing, which she saw as a means of getting in touch with her unconscious. Aside from passing references to "working with my chakras," she didn't say much about the sessions themselves. Instead, she used the journals to record meditations, dreams, and visions. Some of the entries were written; others consisted of paintings and line drawings. The source of Olivia's disappointment must have been that so much of the journals are taken up with Ruth's efforts to imagine what was going on inside herself rather than to record what she was doing and feeling.

It's never very interesting to hear about another person's dreams, and, when my mother was writing, I don't think she had an audience other than herself in mind. At the time she became ill, Ruth was a working musician, and many of her fantasies involve the world of classical music performance and personalities. There are also recurring fantasies about having sex with her doctor, with friends and colleagues, with multiple men, with famous people like Teddy Kennedy and Henry Kissinger, once with a woman, and occasionally with my father. Sexual desire must have seemed as far as she could get from death, pleasure the antithesis of suffering. Sometimes Ruth imagines herself in foreign places far from the shrinking world of home and doctors. She also writes about visions of traveling down into her own body to explore what's going on. There, she meets an Indian woman who is sometimes caring for an older woman or a young child. Ruth joins in, getting intense satisfaction out of rudimentary activities like cooking, cleaning, and washing. In another fantasy, she's conscripted to assist a "mentally defective" young man in a wheelchair. Caring for others is a welcome alternative to the painful decline of her body.

I felt less discouraged by all of this than my sister. As a literary critic, I was trained to find meaning in obscure or evasive texts. Ruth didn't intend for these journals to be read as a linear narrative, and she may not have intended them to be read at all, imagining her writing as a purely therapeutic activity. But they did say more about her experiences than was immediately apparent. The story they told was horrifying. Reading it felt obscene, like I was witness to a spiral of despair and suffering almost too awful to imagine.

As I read the journals, I realized that I didn't know much about Ruth. Nobody who knew her well had made much effort to help my sister and me to preserve her memory. I had only fleeting impressions of my life with her, and most of them involved illness. Paging through the notebooks was like meeting her for the first time. Through her writing, Ruth emerges as a stylish, energetic, and driven woman. She believed that appearances were important, even in the most intimate situations. She took pride in her luxurious, elegantly styled hair, and in never being seen without her eyes romantically lined in kohl. She wore a velvet cape, and was an aficionado of classical music and the arts. She loved order. Ruth believed strongly in the power of self-fashioning, tracing her vivacious personality back to a moment when, at age thirteen, she decided to "stop being an introvert." She was determined to be a good sport, refusing to complain about the skiing and backpacking trips my father loved, no matter how uncomfortable she was. Much of her personality seems to have developed in reaction against her family: a brilliant and cruel brother; a mother who was lazy and unkind, taking to bed for the last decade of her life; and a father whom she describes as distant, boring, and self-centered. Determined not to repeat the mistakes of her own parents, she writes that she was "disbelievingly joyful at having a child" in the months after my birth.

Nothing about her life prepared her for the tragedy that unfolds in the journals.

The first was a gift, a large burgundy book with the words "THE BOOK OF LIFE. Ruth Adams" embossed on the cover. Inside is a handwritten inscription from her best friend, Barbara Myerhoff (who would also die of lung cancer just ten years later). "Please accept this book—for all of us," she writes. I imagined Barbara at age forty, confronting the certain death of her dear friend. She was an anthropologist who strongly believed in the power of magical thinking, and she must have seen writing of dreams and visions as an antidote to Ruth's suffering and grief.

The journals document the intense alienation and loss of illness. A pair of watercolors shows Ruth giving up her career. In the first, her limp body is held up by the members of her chamber music group. Dressed in the long black robes they wore for performance, they look like mourners at a funeral. In the second, the group stands on a brightly lit stage as she walks off into the shadows. Ruth describes how dispiriting it is to list her occupation as "housewife" on medical forms. "Cancer patient isn't a profession," she writes. Isolation is the subject of a painting titled "I alone am sad," where Ruth sits naked and crying under a tree while other families smile and play together, oblivious to her suffering. Over time, Ruth's fear and pain cause her to turn inward, making contact only with her closest friends. She writes of the loss associated with cutting off her luxurious dark hair, the decline of her body, her frustration at being unable to clean and order her daughters' room, and her inability to do the most basic household tasks.

Nowhere does she mention hope for a medical cure. Any talk of healing comes not from medicine but through visions, prayers, and miracle. Her doctors are ignorant and bungling, helpless to stop the course of her illness or provide her much relief from pain. As her disease progresses, she resents the feeling of being in their power. Her treatments, which she often describes as a kind of contamination, are torturous and ultimately futile. In a line drawing called "I reject the poison," Ruth is naked, her back covered in sores as she vomits and throws bottles of pills at a group of doctors. Occasionally she describes her doctor Larry as an object of her sexual fantasies, but more often he is a somewhat pathetic figure, unable to help or understand her suffering. In the last weeks of her life, Larry offers her some red pills that promise to end her misery when it becomes too much to bear. She vacillates between a fierce desire to live and the guarantee of escape held out by the pills. One night her suffering is so intense that she takes a pill. Instead of bringing relief, it makes her feel like she is suffocating, and she spends hours screaming and gasping for breath. Afterward, she is cast into despair to realize that she has no hope of a peaceful end.

I think Olivia was most disappointed that there wasn't more about us in the journals. But we are there. In a drawing called "Rachel's and my shadows meet," Ruth and I are both crying. She's hitting me, as I lie in front of her kicking my legs in a frenzy of rage. In another called "My shadow responds to Olivia's non-accidental loss of her glasses," she appears as an angry giant, looming over a child huddled on the floor. Ruth writes of repeated fantasies in which she tries desperately to get to her children, who are threatened by fires, floods, landslides, and concentration camps. As she watches us playing with the babysitter, she is filled with jealousy at the thought of not being there to see us grow up. We pull her toward life at the moments of greatest agony, and our need for her makes her illness all the more tragic.

As the end approaches, suffering creeps more frequently into her writing. Even when she's describing visions and dreams, she can't avoid mentioning the terrible pain and struggle for breath. She lies awake at night unable to breathe, or wakes screaming and gasping for air. In her last written entry, she's in despair. After finding that the red pills make things worse, she sees no chance for a painless death. In the final paragraph, she turns to a fantasy of escape. "If someone had wound a mile-long black silk sash around my middle, tightly, which would make it hard to breathe, I would have to patiently unwind it, one round at a time. At first, as I wound and wound I wouldn't feel any relief; that would only come bit by bit, but what a feeling!" I was glad that Ruth could imagine an end to her suffering, but I felt devastated by the experience of reading. I thumbed through the remaining blank pages of Ruth's journal, the white space confronting me like all the years of life she had been so unfairly denied. I wondered what it would have been like to know she might not be there to finish her book.

After I finished the journals, I felt haunted. Instead of making me feel better, reading them made things so much worse. It was as if opening the books had released an angry ghost. Everywhere I went, Ruth was there, reminding me that one day I too would be dead. I felt her as I walked down the street using my undiseased lungs to breathe in the ripe smells of Manhattan in the summer. She peered over my shoulder as I tried to read or cook dinner. And she was most definitely there whenever I was with my children. Sometimes there was a sadness about her, but more often she felt malevolent, a restless, jealous ghost who refused to let me forget that life could be short and painful. I sealed the books in a plastic bag and tucked them into the back of my closet, wishing I had never opened them. But I had summoned something up, and hiding the books did nothing to put it back to rest.

On vacation in California later that summer, we went to visit Rachel, a friend I had known since childhood. It made me nervous to see Noah and Henry charging around her beautiful house, even after she insisted that nothing was breakable. Finally they settled at the piano, pounding on the keys and singing tunelessly to each other. When I tried to apologize for the noise, Rachel laughed and reminded me that she had three kids of her own. "Drink this, and stop worrying," she said, pushing a glass of wine into my hand. "I'm going to finish making dinner."

As soon as she left the room, I felt Ruth there. I wasn't surprised. Ruth had been haunting me for months, and it made sense that she would show up to ruin my vacation in southern California, where she had lived and died. I took a deep breath, trying to enjoy the expansion of my healthy lungs and the sight of my children laughing and singing. To my surprise, it worked. I could still feel Ruth there, but she didn't seem angry or envious of my happiness. She seemed restful, approving. I wondered whether it was the piano. Surely my mother the musician would have liked the idea of her grandsons taking such evident pleasure in playing together. My father had tried unsuccessfully to pass along her musical abilities to my sister and me. He took us to concerts and the opera and played classical music records constantly in our home. I had years of piano and violin lessons to no avail. I had a tin ear, and Olivia was only slightly better. But as I watched my sons, I thought that maybe my parents' love of music had skipped a generation.

After that day, I still felt Ruth. Sometimes, I sensed her sadness and envy. But she felt less malevolent, and often she even seemed approving. I wondered whether I had misunderstood, whether there might be another way of explaining why I had summoned her up. Maybe she wasn't there to torment me. Maybe she was there to remind me that she and I are different people. A tragedy happened to her, and, by extension, to me. But it happened a long time ago, and that didn't mean I was fated to come to the same end. Ruth reminded me that life can be short and miserable, but she could just as easily remind me to enjoy its pleasures and rewards. Someone in my family had Down syndrome. We didn't plan for things to happen this way, but our lives weren't tragic. Nobody had cancer, and nobody was planning to die anytime soon.

I thought a lot about Ruth's recurring fantasy of caring for someone—the elderly woman, the child, or the man in a wheelchair. In these visions, she finds satisfaction in basic tasks like growing her own vegetables, preparing food from scratch, cooking, and cleaning. In the midst of her suffering, she longs for an uncomplicated life, driven by basic needs and demands. As I rushed around the noisy streets of Manhattan, busy with my work and my kids, I thought about how far I was from the simple activities my mother dreamed of as she was dying. But in quieter moments I thought again. I had trained my son's eyes to track. I was teaching him to chew, bite by bite. I used my fingers to shape his mouth into the first rudiments of speech. I couldn't imagine tasks more elementary, or more rewarding. Maybe, in the frenetic heart of Manhattan, Henry had brought me to the simple place my mother always longed to reach.

A Simple Place

Finding a Voice

I WAS ALWAYS DISTURBED BY the silence of freaks. In a traditional sideshow, the performers sat mutely on their platforms while customers pointed and stared. There is a memorable scene in Carson McCullers's novel *Member of the Wedding* where the protagonist, twelve-year-old Frankie Addams, goes to see the freaks at the state fair. As they gaze at her she feels afraid, imagining they can understand her innermost secrets. And who can say otherwise? Because the freaks don't talk, it's easy for Frankie to project her deepest fears and anxieties onto them. But I doubt they were thinking of her at all, let alone capable of reading her mind. As I researched my book, I was delighted when I found evidence of performers talking back at the spectators who provoked them. After hours of being stared at, insulted, and sometimes poked by curious onlookers, their frustration must have boiled over. In those moments, freaks remind us that they aren't mirrors reflecting the fears and desires of the "normals" who pay to gawk at them. They can't peer into the depths of our souls. In fact, most of them care very little about the bland, anonymous folk who parade through the tent day after day. They are performers with a job to do. But before that, they are people, with ordinary human needs, thoughts, and feelings of their own.

Without their words, how would we know any of this? My research made me realize how important it was for people with disabilities to speak for themselves. One reason for the decline of freak shows was a growing recognition that it wasn't right to turn people into voiceless objects just because their bodies looked different. As freak shows began to wane over the course of the twentieth century, showmen were replaced by doctors who used the language of medicine rather than curiosity to define the freak's body. But that shift did little to improve the lives of people with disabilities, who found doctors no less exploitative than sideshow managers. When the movement for disability rights emerged in the 1970s and 1980s, one of its slogans was "Nothing About Us Without Us." The idea was that people with disabilities had been silent for too long. They were tired of being spoken for by others, no matter how well intentioned, and they demanded to be included in decisions about their own lives. Everywhere I looked, I found examples of the connection between voice and self-determination. There was a UNICEF campaign inviting people to "speak out on disability rights." "Hear our voices" was the rallying cry of the Disability Rights Fund. An activist group in California called itself SpeakOut! The self-advocacy movement announced how important it was for people with intellectual disabilities to learn to "speak up for ourselves."

All of this made me aware of how crucial speech would be to Henry's future. No matter how capable he was, his opportunities would be limited if he couldn't speak for himself. And it was quickly becoming apparent that speech would be his biggest challenge. He was doing beautifully in all the other domains of early intervention. Thanks to Joy, his physical development had taken off. Henry was walking, climbing, throwing, and catching. He wrestled vigorously with Noah, eager to copy his big brother's every move. He was working on drawing, cutting, and threading beads onto a string with his occupational therapists. With Alison's help, he was able to do puzzles, match colors, and play with dolls. The patience and ingenuity of our feeding therapist was also paying off, and he had started to eat table food along with the rest of us. He could even feed himself with a fork and spoon.

For a while, Henry's speech seemed to be coming along too. In the summer before he started at the Family Center he could say "up" when he wanted to get out of his high chair, he had an impressive repertoire of animal noises, and he was developing a healthy ability to say "no" to nearly every situation. Along with his verbal speech, he had a growing vocabulary of sign language. Jackie had explained the importance of sign, which works out of the same area of the brain as speech. Sign allows children with verbal delays to develop vocabulary and communication skills, even when spoken language lags far behind. Once he got the hang of it, Henry learned new signs easily and used them enthusiastically to express himself and tell us things about the world. He loved to sit with his books, looking at the pictures and making the signs we had taught him. All of this appeared to be a promising start down the road to spoken language.

Then Henry's words disappeared. He continued to sign, but his spoken words were gone. All of them. During the fall, his teachers and therapists were reassuring. His physical development was racing ahead, which often causes speech to go dormant, they told us. As soon as he got really comfortable walking, his words would come back just as suddenly as they had vanished. But months went by, and all we heard was a constant soundtrack of open vowels. Henry's walking became steady and confident. He even started learning to ride a bike, which Joy had equipped with a handle and straps to hold his feet onto the pedals. Still, everything was accompanied by a steady stream of "ahh" sounds. Consonants like "b" and "m" didn't come out unless actively prompted by his speech therapists. When I tried to copy what they had done, I had very little success. And no words at all.

What made this all the more frustrating was that Henry had such a good grasp of spoken communication. One of the ways we knew this was his puppet shows. Just around his second birthday, Henry fell in love with puppets. He liked Sesame Street characters best, but he wasn't picky. Sometimes even a sock or a plain paper bag would do. He liked to put one puppet on each hand, allowing them to talk animatedly to each other. Their gestures and inflections and the quality of give and take between them showed a very perceptive understanding of how dialogue works. So perceptive that people would stop to watch as Henry wheeled down the street in his stroller, one puppet talking in animated jargon to the other. Sometimes a small crowd would gather around us on the subway platform. Henry, who normally loved an audience, would be so absorbed in the conversation between Elmo and Big Bird, or Ernie and Bert, that he didn't even notice. Of course, we couldn't understand what the puppets were saying with such urgency and excitement. We would have given anything to know what was going on in Henry's mind, and what those puppets were talking about. Much as I loved to see Henry so perfectly imitating the patterns of verbal speech, I also knew we needed to do everything possible to enable him to tell us.

I arranged to sit in on one of Jackie's sessions at the Family Center. As I watched her work with Henry, I started to see a disturbing pattern. It wasn't that Henry didn't understand language. I could tell he knew what was being asked of him. If Jackie wanted him to match two pictures or point to something red, he could do it. I also saw him trying hard to speak. But it was as if his mouth couldn't form the words he wanted to say. When Jackie directed him to say "up," which he had done so beautifully and clearly the summer before, it came out "pa." When she blew bubbles and prompted him to say "pop," Henry said "da." The next time they tried it, he said "ba." He was clearly regressing, having lost words he was able to say only a few months before and seemingly unable to control the sounds coming out of his mouth. I could tell that Jackie was frustrated, and I felt a mounting sense of despair. When the session ended, she told me she thought he had apraxia of speech, a disorder that makes it difficult to form words consistently and clearly. "The good news is that the treatment is exactly the same," she said. "Apraxia is just a description of what's happening with Henry. We won't do anything differently, but it will help us to understand why he's struggling."

Nothing about this sounded like good news to me. I left the Family Center filled with anxiety. There was always something. Every time Henry appeared to be making progress, we hit another stumbling block. Now, on top of the ordinary speech delays associated with Down syndrome, he would have apraxia to contend with. And of all possible types of delay, speech seemed like the worst. We didn't care if Henry became a talented athlete, or if he could play classical guitar. But we were a family whose lives revolved around words. The ability to communicate was essential to my career and my sense of self. I was a writer, but the way I developed my ideas was by talking about them with other people. I shared my finished work by giving talks at conferences and universities. I loved giving lectures, answering questions, the give and take of a seminar. I took great satisfaction from knowing I had explained a concept or an idea clearly, realizing I had taught something to my students or changed the way they thought about a problem. What would Henry's future be like if he had no voice?

As I always did in moments of doubt, I went home and started to read. I knew that "praxis" meant action or planned movement. I learned that "apraxia" (also known as "dyspraxia") is a motor planning disorder, a kind of loose wiring that makes it difficult for the brain to communicate with the mouth. Like an ailing flashlight, one moment the connection may work just fine, the next it's lost and you're left in the dark. People with apraxia find it difficult to direct their mouths to make sounds correctly, and to put sounds and syllables together. Long words are harder than short ones. They also have trouble with inflection, the subtle changes in pitch and tone that come naturally to most speakers. Their mistakes are inconsistent, so one day they may struggle mightily to make a sound that came easily the day before. In children with apraxia, expressive language, the ability to communicate, lags far behind receptive language, the ability to understand. As Jackie had explained, the recommended treatment was the same kind of regular and sustained therapy Henry was already receiving.

I also learned that because speech delays are so common in children with Down syndrome, apraxia tends to get overlooked. The inability to speak is often mistaken for low intelligence, and the condition goes untreated. I took it as evidence of Jackie's regard for Henry that she recognized apraxia at such a young age. Even in typically developing children, apraxia isn't usually detected until they reach preschool. When Henry was just a little older than two, Jackie realized the specific nature of his problems had to do with a short circuit between his brain and his mouth. She knew he could understand far more than he could stay, and she also saw how motivated he was to speak. He didn't get discouraged when he made mistakes or couldn't

Finding a Voice

be understood. These were all positive signs that he might be able to overcome his difficulties. Jackie had always believed in Henry, finding hope in the slightest sign of progress. But much as I appreciated the affirmation, I felt discouraged by having a new mountain to climb.

It didn't help that Henry's other speech therapist disagreed with Jackie on nearly everything. Ellen had been treating Henry since he started going to daycare. Because of his speech delays, we had been given a generous allotment of early intervention, which covered three sessions with Jackie at the Family Center and three at home with Ellen. I liked Ellen very much, and I trusted her opinions. When we first met, I was immediately struck by how well organized and professional she was. I appreciated her calm and pleasant manner, and her willingness to give clear explanations for what she was doing. I also liked that she seemed close to Jackie in her philosophy and methods. Before she started working with Henry she outlined the approach she would take, and it sounded consistent with what he was already doing. During Henry's short life I had learned that speech and language pathologists are the most tribal of therapists. There are strongly divergent beliefs about how to treat a child with symptoms like Henry's, and I had spent a good deal of time trying to research and understand the different approaches to make sure our therapists were giving him what he needed. If Henry was going to have two speech therapists, it seemed crucial for them to have consistent ideas about his treatment.

But once the two therapists got to work, disagreements started to emerge. For experts in communication, they seemed surprisingly reluctant to communicate with each other, leaving me to observe and do my best to report to each therapist what the other was doing. Jackie used an approach called "total communication" that involved multiple forms of expression. The theory was that alternative forms of communication like sign and pictures activate the same areas of the brain as verbal speech. By combining them, the therapist could offer a child with speech delays many different ways to communicate. The methods were eclectic, determined by the needs and abilities of each particular child. When she worked with Henry, Jackie combined "oral motor stimulation" (massaging his face and the inside of his mouth), sign language, gestures, and PROMPT, a technique that involved guiding the mouth into producing a desired sound. She and Henry took turns blowing bubbles while she prompted him to say "bubbles," "more," and "pop." As they read a book, she asked him to name the animals and the sounds they made. When they ate a snack together, she shaped Henry's mouth to say things like "give me," "more," "mmmm," "good," and "all done." PROMPT is supposed to be an especially good method for treating apraxia because it gives direction to a mouth that is uncertain about what to do with itself. The idea is that gradually the mouth builds motor pathways that allow it to more effortlessly remember how to make particular sounds.

Ellen also used PROMPT, and she also built Henry's speech therapy around playful activities with books, puppets, and snacks. But that was where the similarities ended. Ellen didn't believe in using sign language to teach speech. We had spent two years teaching Henry to sign, and his vocabulary continued to grow as he worked with Jackie at school. The problem with this, Ellen told me, is that most people don't know sign. As Henry grew up and became more independent, he would need to be able to communicate in a way that everybody could understand. No matter how articulate he was at sign, it was unlikely that the ordinary person on the street would know what he was trying to say. Ellen began to discourage Henry's signs by not returning them and prompting him to speak instead. She also started to advocate for an alternative communication system. This might be as simple as a picture board, which would allow Henry to point to the things he wanted to say. It could also be an electronic device with a recorded voice that would speak for him. These alternatives were better, Ellen claimed, because anybody could understand them. "Using a device can also take the pressure off," she told us. "Once a child doesn't feel compelled to speak, language sometimes comes in more quickly."

Ellen's arguments sounded convincing to me, especially when I was talking to her. But when I was talking to Jackie, I felt equally convinced that she was right. I was dismayed to find myself in the middle of a disagreement I felt unqualified to resolve. It seemed to me that each therapist had valid points. My reading suggested that sign language did stimulate the same area of the brain as verbal speech, and that children who used sign actually learned to speak just as well as, if not better than, those who didn't. But I also realized the limitations of sign as a long-term method of communication. What if Henry got to kindergarten and his teacher didn't know sign? We would have to start all over again from scratch. Why not start now with a system that was accessible to everyone? Because, Jackie argued, a device, especially an electronic one, would be an alternative to verbal speech. It would be like a crutch that Henry might learn to use instead of talking. Total communication involved the entire body, whereas a device was likely to impede, rather than encourage, other ways of speaking.

I should have been more comfortable with this dispute. In my professional world, literary critics thrive on conflict and debate. Ask ten critics to read the same book and each one will come up with a different analysis that she'll fight to the death to defend. Our originality rests on finding flaws in the arguments other people have already made, then staking out a unique and original way of looking at something familiar. That's why, when I type "Moby Dick" into the library database, more than 850 articles and 361 books come up. But Henry wasn't a book, he was my child. If I wrote an interpretation of *Moby-Dick* and then I decided I was mistaken, I could always change my mind and write something else. With Henry, we had only one chance. And the decisions we made mattered so much. Much as I loved my work, I knew that nobody's life hung in the balance because of it. But the choices we made about Henry's speech therapy could mean the difference between whether or not he arrived at kindergarten able to communicate with his teachers and peers.

I could see Ellen's point that alternative communication was more easily understood than sign language. But I hated the idea of a device. I worried that she didn't believe Henry would ever speak clearly enough to communicate. When I asked her directly, she was noncommittal, saying she had no way to predict what Henry would be able to do in the future. All she could do was to base her plan of treatment on where he was now. But I thought that if she really believed he had a chance to communicate verbally, she wouldn't be proposing use of the device. And even if I had any enthusiasm for the idea, Jackie was totally opposed. She had never used an electronic device and she didn't intend to start. I worried that if we were to get a device, Henry might be confused if Jackie used one method at school, and Ellen did something else at home. Not knowing what else to do, I did nothing. I didn't tell Ellen that an alternative communication system was out of the question, but I didn't make any effort to move ahead with one either.

As time went on and Henry made so little progress, I started to think more seriously about the alternatives. A friend's son got a device, and she reported that it had made a big difference. I also realized that our early intervention services were coming to an end. Ellen was an early intervention therapist, and she would leave us when Henry aged out of the program. When he turned three, six months down the road, we would have to start all over again with services administered by the board of education, which was much slower and less generous about granting requests for equipment. If we decided Henry needed a device at some later point, it would be harder to get funding to buy it and pay for training. Not wanting to miss our window of opportunity, we finally decided to get Henry evaluated by a specialist in alternative communication.

As soon as I met Tricia, our evaluator, I started to think we had made the right decision. I found it hard not to share her enthusiasm as she talked excitedly about the possibilities a device would open up. After showing Henry several different models, Tricia thought a machine called a TechSpeak would be perfect, and she promised to meet with us several times to show us how to use it. The TechSpeak was a simple keyboard with picture buttons that could be programmed with recorded words. When Tricia described how Henry would use this device and what it would do for him, I felt completely persuaded. She explained that it wouldn't be an alternative to spoken communication but a way to enhance and supplement existing speech. As Henry got used to his device, it would support, rather than discourage, verbal speech. If the words were recorded by someone important to him, like a parent or sibling, that would be all the more incentive for him to speak. Not only would he try to imitate the sounds it was making, but he would also be able to develop an understanding of more complex multiword expressions. Although apraxia limited him to the one-syllable words his mouth could form, it was clear that he was capable of saying so much more if only his mouth would cooperate. The device would enable Henry to say those things, making it more likely that his ability to express himself would keep up with his ability to understand. What I liked best of all was that Tricia had evidence to back up her claims. She sent me a pile of articles describing the current research on augmentative communications devices, all of it supporting her argument that they enhanced, rather than delayed, the development of verbal speech.

Once we put in the order, it took quite a while for our own TechSpeak to arrive. By that time, Henry had only a few weeks left in early intervention. Tricia came to our apartment to show me how to design sheets of buttons that went with different activities and program the device to make sound. Henry would need constant supervision, she told us, to ensure that he was using it only to communicate. It should never be treated as a toy. We practiced a few very simple exercises. In theory these would get more complicated as Henry's understanding grew and he became familiar with the device. Once again, I found myself caught up in Tricia's excitement. I saw the potential and I thought Henry would love working with it. But it was also clear to me that it would be impossible to use correctly without the help of someone who had experience and training. Ellen had both, but we had only a few more sessions left with her, and then a long summer vacation before Henry started with his new speech therapist in the fall. The only hope for any continuity was to get Jackie on board, since she would continue to see Henry at the Family Center after he segued into the preschool room.

When Jackie saw the device, she was dismissive. "It does exactly the same things I'm already doing with Henry," she said, shaking her head. "But instead of being inspired to speak, he'll be pushing buttons. He's going to be distracted. I think it will shut down rather than develop his words."

Still, she agreed to use it for a few minutes in each session, and we started to bring it along when Henry went to the Family Center. At first, she reported, her predictions were confirmed. She said that Henry fell silent when he was using the device. Often he just wanted to play with it, pushing the buttons to hear the sounds rather than to communicate. It seemed no better to her than the activities she had already designed to prompt Henry's speech. But over time, something happened. As the device became less new and exciting, Henry started using it to communicate. And as he did, Jackie started to see its benefits and to make it a more serious part of her sessions. She asked me to make keypads for new activities. She wanted to be put in touch with Tricia to learn more about what could be done with the device. The next thing I knew, she was using it with other children in the program, and even recommending it to their parents.

After a year with the TechSpeak, Henry had a lot more verbal language. He could say quite a few words, and lot more things that sounded like words even if we couldn't understand them. It was still hard for him to put two words together, and it was still clear that he understood a lot more than he could say. We would never know for sure whether the TechSpeak had anything to do with his progress.

As Tricia described it to me, the TechSpeak would become a part of Henry's daily life. He would carry it with him and use it in a variety of different situations. At mealtimes, the TechSpeak would guide him to request different foods and tell us when he wanted more and when he was finished. At play, it would help him to communicate what he wanted and what he was doing. There were also exercises to do when we were reading books or playing games, which would allow us to talk about what he saw and understood. As he grew up, the boards could become more sophisticated, evolving along with his ability for complex thought.

In reality, that wasn't what happened. The device was too cumbersome. Each activity required a different sheet of buttons, which had to be designed using a special computer program. The sheets had to be printed in color and laminated, and they took time to load and unload. Henry couldn't change the boards himself. He also wasn't allowed to have the device unless an adult was monitoring him. This made it impossible to use for any kind of spontaneous speech. I found it hard to remember to bring it to the Family Center each morning and remind Angela to pick it up at the end of the day. So we started to leave it there during the week, and then for weeks at a stretch. We didn't miss it at home. There really was no way to use it there, since it worked best for more structured activities of the kind Henry was doing at school or in therapy. I no longer had anything against the device. It just wasn't practical. I thought that maybe one day when Henry was older and more mature, he might use some form of augmentative communication on his own. I realized I no longer felt like this would be a tragedy, because the device had made me think differently about what it meant to speak.

Of course, even before I met the TechSpeak, I knew that communication wasn't only about the ability to use verbal language. But after the device entered our lives, I had the somewhat ironic insight, given that I'm a writer, that I had privileged the spoken word over all other forms of communication. What I came to understand may sound obvious. Those slogans about speaking up and learning to speak for yourself had very little to do with being able to talk. Some people talk; others may have just as much to say using sign, body language, and assistive communication devices. Important as it was for Henry to learn to talk to the best of his ability, it was just as important that I accept all these ways of communicating as legitimate forms of speech. As the TechSpeak faded from our daily life, we continued to hope Henry would be able to talk clearly in a way that others could understand, and to do everything we could to make that possible. But at the same time, I had come to acknowledge that speech wasn't the only genuine means of self-expression. I believed that one day Henry would have a voice, and he would be able to speak for himself. Whether it would come from a mechanical device, a picture card, or his own mouth, it was too early to tell.

The Girl Down the Street

MORE THAN ONE MEMOIR ABOUT Down syndrome tells the story of the vanishing obstetrician. Having delivered a baby so immediately and evidently imperfect, she doesn't know what to do. Apparently, abandoning your patient at a moment of postpartum crisis isn't covered by the Hippocratic oath. So she simply leaves the room, never to reappear.

My obstetrician didn't vanish. Dr. Lewis wasn't there at the birth, but she did surface two days later to tell me she was sorry. What she offered me—the story of the girl with Down syndrome who played with all the other children on the block—gave little comfort. But for reasons I can't quite explain, I continued to see her for my annual checkups. Her care continued to be cheery and mechanical. Despite all we had been through, she expressed little interest in me or my children, beyond the most perfunctory "and how are the kids?" I would lie there with my legs in stirrups, twitching with resentment and resolving never to return. But for several years I did. I went partly out of inertia. Henry filled my life so completely that my own medical care seemed like an afterthought. But I also went back out of an odd sense of gratitude. I knew that, however flawed her bedside manner, Dr. Lewis enabled the choices that led to Henry's birth. And by the time my first yearly pelvic exam rolled around, I couldn't imagine my life without him.

I knew how rare it was to find an obstetrician like Dr. Lewis in Manhattan, where, for women of a certain age, amnio is presented less as an option than a routine aspect of prenatal care. I had heard of parents who had to fight their doctors to decline testing. Others, who had received a positive diagnosis of Down syndrome, had to fight to give birth to their babies. I was grateful to have escaped all of that. It was shocking enough to learn that our new baby had Down syndrome. I couldn't imagine having to wrestle with the question of whether he should be born at all, especially in the face of a doctor's disapproval.

When Henry turned two, I wrote Dr. Lewis a card, telling her how much I appreciated this aspect of her care. When it came to prenatal testing, I could tell she believed her patients should make their own choices, free of a doctor's judgment. By then I felt differently about the story of her neighbors, which had seemed so insulting at the time. I decided it was her way of saying, however imperfectly, that having a child with Down syndrome wasn't a devastating tragedy, as so many other doctors seemed to believe. I put some photos of Henry in the envelope and asked her to hang them in her office, along with pictures of all the other children she had brought into the world.

When I went to my next appointment, the pictures were there on the wall. Dr. Lewis didn't mention the letter or ask about my children. Instead, she talked about her son's college applications while she poked around inside me. She hoped he would go to Columbia, but was trying to remain impartial. She didn't ask to see the new pictures I had tucked into my bag the night before. On my way out, I left them with her assistant, who promised to add them to the wall.

The Girl Down the Street

A week later, our Down syndrome parent group organized an outing, and we offered a ride to a mother and son who had just moved to our neighborhood. At some point during the long drive, I learned that Dr. Lewis had also been her obstetrician.

"I don't see her anymore," Natalia said decisively. "Let's just say she wasn't very supportive."

I said I was surprised. Much as I disliked Dr. Lewis, she seemed to offer her patients a wide range of options about their pregnancies, and seemed willing to support them in whatever choices they made.

Then again, Natalia's situation was very different from mine. Her screening indicated a strong likelihood of Down syndrome, later confirmed by an amnio. "At that point, she told me about her neighbor," Natalia said.

I nodded. Of course I remembered the neighbor, the girl with Down syndrome who played with all the other kids.

But Natalia wasn't finished. "She said the girl was always running away. It was awful. Her parents couldn't control her and she kept getting lost. They had to call the police to help find her. She made their lives miserable.

"She told me that story more than once," Natalia continued. "Along with a lot of other terrible things. Because she thought it was a mistake for me to give birth to this baby when I didn't have to. She said he would be a burden. She wanted me to, you know." She let her voice trail off, aware of Noah listening to every word.

I thought about the card, the pictures on the wall, Dr. Lewis's tears in the hospital. Suddenly it all looked very different. Her tears were real, but not for the reason I had imagined. I thought she was crying because she was sorry for my grief and worry, but it must have been because she was sorry my baby had been born. Like so many other doctors, she believed he was a mistake that should have been prevented, a case of medical science gone wrong.

I didn't quite know how to take this revelation. Jon likes to call me "the elephant of wrongs," the person who never forgets a slight or disagreement. I expected to feel angry and betrayed. But I didn't feel much of anything. I wondered if I was in shock. I thought that maybe the presence of Natalia and her son in the car was preventing me from getting at my feelings. Maybe later I would cry and rage at being betrayed by someone who had turned out to be a very different person from the one I thought I knew.

As we drove home, I continued to feel very little. If I felt anything, it was relief. Natalia's story had given me a reason never to see Dr. Lewis again. With that realization, I understood that a chapter in my past had come to a close. Somewhere in the frenetic rush of my life, the drama of Henry's birth, the constant need to relive decisions about testing and the other circumstances that brought him into the world, had ended. I couldn't say when it had happened, or why. But the emotions that would have made this story so earth-shattering just simply weren't there anymore. All that was left was my appreciation for its literary merits, the perfect combination of coincidence, suspense, and reversal that made it better than any fiction I could have dreamed up.

The car lapsed into silence. Everybody was tired out by the day's activities, and I couldn't think of anything more to say. Eventually, Jon spoke up. He thought he had missed our exit and asked me to help navigate. I looked for the directions, which had fallen under his seat. Henry was behind me, absorbed in a Sesame Street DVD. As I reached back, he caught my eye and his face lit up with a smile that engaged his whole body. I smiled too, and turned to the map of the road ahead.

Surprised by Disability

IN MY QUEST TO LEARN as much as I could, I had joined two other women for a conference called Best Practices in Education of Children with Down Syndrome. It was way out on Long Island, impossible to reach without a car. When my friend Joanna offered me a ride, I jumped at the chance. Another mom named Sophie and her baby son Jonah came along with us. The conference program looked promising, with panels on speech therapy, literacy, and inclusive education. But I was most interested in the keynote presentations. These would be delivered by two young adults with Down syndrome, the actor Ashley Wolfe and the musician Sujeet Desai. By that point, I knew a lot of children with Down syndrome but still hadn't managed to meet many adults. Seeing adults with Down syndrome had become incredibly important to me, and I was dismayed by how hard it was to find them. Jon and I wondered how there could be so many children in our lives, and so few teens or adults. What happened to them? Why weren't they visible in public? Where did they go? I became a Down syndrome stalker. If I glimpsed a person with Down syndrome on the street, I would follow her with my eyes, wondering what she was capable of, what she liked doing, whether she had a happy life. Sometimes I would even walk behind her for a block or so. One night Jon and I saw two women with Down syndrome in a restaurant where we were having dinner. We spent the rest of the meal craning our necks, trying to see what they were doing. There was no clear goal to my spying, except that I felt irresistibly curious about the lives of adults with Down syndrome. Of course I knew that every person was different. A random adult on the street told me very little about what Henry might become, especially given the vast improvements in therapy and health care available to his generation. But those chance encounters helped me to think about possible futures that otherwise seemed so difficult to imagine.

The presentations by Ashley Wolfe and Sujeet Desai promised a more sustained look at what it meant to be an adult with Down syndrome. During the ride out to Long Island, Joanna, Sophie, and I talked about preschool, therapy, our kids' progress with eating and speech. On the way back, we talked about what we had seen and heard at the conference. We all agreed that the sessions were of mixed quality, some being very informative and others plodding and unorganized. When we got into Manhattan, Joanna offered to drive us to her apartment, which was near a subway that would take Sophie and me the rest of the way home. As we walked to the train, Sophie confessed her disappointment with the keynote speakers. Ashley's presentation had been funny and charming, but she seemed confused when I tried to talk to her afterward. Sophie had watched our stilted exchange with dismay, wondering why it was so hard for Ashley to respond to a basic social interaction.

And Sujeet Desai wasn't much of a musician. Sure, he could play the clarinet, Sophie said, but there was a recorded accompaniment playing in the background, and his mother had to take care of the microphone and his video presentation. I felt much more positive about what I had seen and heard. Both Ashley and Sujeet seemed quite capable to me. They spoke clearly, interacted warmly with their parents, and had passions that gave them happiness and satisfaction. This seemed like the best any mother could hope for her child. As we debated the merits of the keynotes, our conversation turned to our own children. That was when Sophie told me she had considered plastic surgery for her son Jonah.

I had learned about "facial reconstruction" from a film I had seen a few months before. It followed two families— one in England, the other in Texas—who decided to normalize the appearance of their children with Down syndrome. They would use procedures first promoted in the 1970s, when surgeons decided it might be a good idea to "correct" the facial features associated with Down syndrome. Although this kind of surgery has always been controversial, even today a quick web search turns up plenty of doctors who continue to offer their services. In the film, the families visit doctors who catalogue each child's features, pointing out abnormalities in need of repair. According to the experts, the British girl needed to be cured of a protruding tongue, floppy ears, and upwardly slanted eyes, each of which required a separate procedure. The boy from Texas would have one lengthy surgery to remove fat from his eyes and cheeks, and add extra bone to his nose. The footage of the surgical procedures was gruesome. I was sickened by the sight of instruments slicing and peeling away skin, laying bare meaty red flesh, sucking out fat, and sewing body parts roughly into position. When the children awoke swathed in bandages, they suffered agonizing pain, made all the worse by their inability to understand what had happened to them. The filmmakers revisited each child several months later, only to find that neither surgery had been entirely successful, leaving mistakes that needed further repairs. Nonetheless, each set of parents remained stubbornly convinced of the rightness of their decision. Faced with an intolerant world, they clung to the idea that normalizing their children's appearance would give them the best chance of being accepted.

Sophie said much the same to me. "Jonah will have enough challenges in life as it is. Shouldn't I give him the chance to look normal?"

I was speechless. While watching the film, I had cried with rage at the ignorance of the parents, and the barbarism of the surgery itself. I was disturbed to hear them talk about Down syndrome as if it were a sickness that required treatment, and the procedures as a necessary cure. I couldn't believe that someone I knew would even think about subjecting her child to such unnecessary suffering. Under ordinary circumstances, I would do anything to avoid a conflict. But this was different. I turned on Sophie, unable to control myself. "I think that's repellant!" I said vehemently, spitting the words out as if they were a bad taste in my mouth.

"Why?" she asked me, her eyes widening. Her tone was genuine. "I can't change the way other people think. But I can give Jonah a chance. What's wrong with that?"

"What's wrong with it?" I could hear my voice getting unattractively shrill as we stood there on the crowded subway platform. "What's wrong with it is that Down syndrome isn't a disease that needs to be cured. The problem is with the world, not our kids. It doesn't help to try to pass them off as something they aren't. I want to change the way other people think. I want to change the world."

Sophie's face fell. "I get it. You think you have it all figured out," she said softly. "You know what I think? I think you have no idea how it is for a person like me. You've had time to understand what it means to be disabled. You've had a whole career. You've been writing about these things for years."

Her voice trembled. "I don't know what I'm doing. I never thought about disability until a few months ago. I never imagined I would have a person with a disability in my family. I don't know what's right for Jonah. I'm trying to learn as best I can. I'm still trying to make sense of things."

I heard what she was saying, and I knew I had been unfair. It was true that I had the good fortune of years of thinking and research to help me make sense of Henry, and to integrate him into my view of the world. Then again, no amount of academic training can prepare you to become the mother of a child with Down syndrome. I didn't know everything. But Sophie was right that I had more tools in my arsenal. Most parents who discover that their new baby has Down syndrome have probably never given a thought to disability until it arrived into their families. Learning how to cope is inevitably a process of trial and error. There is no right way to do it.

"Jonah is just so beautiful the way he is," I said more gently, reaching over to stroke his cheek. I meant it. More than one passenger on the train had smiled admiringly at his blue button eyes and halo of blond hair. "Why would you want him to be any different? Don't you at least want to try to make the world a better place for him to live in?"

By the time Sophie and Jonah had to change trains, the tension had dissipated. But our confrontation got me thinking about who I was before Henry was born and how much I had changed since he came into our lives. It wasn't just the upheavals in my daily routines. It was a dramatic reorientation of my intellectual life, whatever traces of it hadn't been obliterated by the therapy and the paperwork and the appointments, not to mention the more ordinary grind of raising two young children.

Surprised by Disability

As a graduate student, I was drawn to freaks because they're rebels and misfits in a society that pushes us into neatly assigned boxes. Unless we belong to a category, we simply don't make sense to others. Are you human or animal? Friend or stranger? Man or woman? Gay or straight? Black or white? Liberal or conservative? Resident or alien? Claiming membership in these groups is a prerequisite for inhabiting the social world. But categories are also always imperfect. Labels made me uncomfortable because I never felt like I really fit in anywhere. Freaks spoke to my own sense of being an outsider. Although I wasn't much of a rebel myself, I felt drawn to their rebelliousness, their refusal (or inability) to live by the rules or accept the social norms that governed the world beyond the sideshow. As any misfit knows, group identities not only tell us who belongs but whom to exclude. A community has to have boundaries separating self from other. As someone who was often dejectedly shut out, I was attracted to the person who would deliberately choose not to fit in. Freaks are the ultimate outsiders, one of a kind. Otherwise, who would pay to see them?

Freaks excel at category confusion, inhabiting the impossible zone between seemingly opposed poles of identity. At the sideshow, it was possible to be both man and woman, animal and human, savage and civilized. As freaks blurred these crucial dividing lines, they helped to reassure paying customers of their own normality. The sideshow platform was the physical manifestation of a more existential division between insiders and outsiders. Being on the normal side of the line was especially important during the great waves of immigration in the late nineteenth and early twentieth centuries, when many of the foreign-born desperately wanted to pass as American. But freaks were also deeply disturbing because they reminded the spectator of all the ways she wasn't quite normal. Maybe her deviance wasn't as visible as that of the freaks on display, but seeing them might spark a twinge of nervous recognition. Audiences couldn't get enough of Albert-Alberta, the half-man, half-woman; Percilla the Monkey Girl, whose body was covered in thick black hair; Prince Randian the human torso; fat ladies; human skeletons; and Zebra People with skin a piebald of black and white. These performers embodied a category confusion that was at once terrifying and too thrilling to be missed.

Along the way to writing my book, I learned a lot about disability. Not all freaks were disabled, but many of the most famous were. Being a "born freak" was a badge of honor. Disability distinguished the real stars from the more interchangeable "working acts," like snake charmers, sword swallowers, and contortionists. Anybody could get a tattoo, but only a select few were born with bodies truly extraordinary enough to draw a crowd. The most sought-after performers had multiple talents, but they also had sensational bodies: the conjoined twins, Chang and Eng; the tiny Tom Thumb and Lavinia Warren; the giant Robert Wadlow; JoJo the Dog-Faced Boy, whose face was covered in silky brown hair; the pinheads Zip and Pip. Their images decorated colorful banners enticing audiences into the show. They sold souvenir portraits and pamphlets containing their life stories. Long after these performers died, their images would linger, a reminder of the remarkable diversity of the human body.

Before the rise of the welfare state, freak shows were a harbor for severely disabled people who often had no other way to make a living. Some performers became rich and famous, traveling the world before settling into comfortable retirement. Chang and Eng became wealthy planters, who owned slaves to work their adjoining estates in North Carolina. They divided their time between separate households, where each had his own wife and children. Other freak performers were cruelly exploited and enjoyed none of the profits of their hard work. They simply had nowhere else to go. I found the story of the conjoined twins Violet and Daisy Hilton especially poignant. When they were babies, their mother sold them to a couple who trained them for a stage career, but also physically abused them and kept them virtual prisoners. As adults, the sisters gained their freedom and earned a living performing on vaudeville and in film. They longed for love and companionship, but their various attempts at marriage ended quickly and unhappily. After being abandoned by their manager, they were forced to take a job as checkers in a local grocery store. They died of the flu alone in their apartment, and their bodies were discovered only after they failed to show up for work. I was haunted by the story of the Hilton sisters. It was a good reality check, reminding me to resist allowing my view of the freak show to be colored by romance. For every disabled performer who earned fame and fortune, many others suffered mightily.

My research on freaks brought me into the world of disability studies, a field that was just entering the humanities when I was a graduate student. I quickly discovered that most scholars of disability studies hated freak shows, seeing them as one of many sad chapters in the history of people with disabilities in the Western world. Disability scholars and activists rejected the idea that disability was a problem with individual bodies that were sick or defective. Rather than fixating on illness or impairment, they were concerned with the environmental factors that excluded some bodies from full participation in the social world. A person in a wheelchair was disabled by stairs and broken elevators, hot by her inability to walk. People with autism were disabled by overstimulating or unfamiliar settings, while deaf people were disabled in a context where verbal language was the only way to communicate. Activists focused not on correcting or curing a given impairment (as doctors are so eager to do) but on removing barriers that made the built environment inaccessible to people with disabilities. This was the goal of the 1990 Americans with Disabilities Act, which gave people with disabilities the right to access schools, businesses, public transportation, and public space. They demanded an end to the warehousing of the disabled in hospitals and institutions. They decried the segregation of disabled children in public schools. And they called for the right to make decisions about their own care and well-being.

I had no quarrel with any of this. In fact, I couldn't have agreed more with the direction that disability studies was taking or the agenda of the disability rights movement. I firmly believed that people with disabilities had a right to equal access, and that all people, including the able-bodied, had something to gain from the changes mandated by the ADA. It was just that my heart wasn't in it. The movement for disability rights was all about accommodation, mainstreaming, inclusion. I'm not proud to say it, but I was much more excited by stories of the people who never wanted to fit in. Instead of trying to become like everybody else, freaks make themselves as strange as possible. For those who were proud of their sensational bodies, circuses, sideshows, and carnivals could be a haven where otherness was the norm and the rules of respectable society didn't apply. Instead of demanding to participate in the world of the able-bodied, freaks helped us imagine how the world could be a radically different place.

The freak's rebellious individuality conflicted with the idea of disabled identity coming out of the movement for disability rights. Historically, people with disabilities have been treated as isolated cases or grouped together according to diagnosis, making it difficult for a wheelchair user to imagine common ground with a blind person, a person with an intellectual disability, or one with a chronic illness. The ADA grew out of the recognition that people with disabilities shared experiences of prejudice and exclusion that transcended their individual differences. Organizing themselves under the banner of disabled identity, people with disabilities became a powerful minority group, second only to women in number. I could understand the political importance of claiming disability as an identity. But I was irresistibly drawn to the freaks who rejected identity altogether. At the sideshow, people with disabilities, people of color, people from exotic parts of the world, and people with exceptional talents were all lumped together as freaks. In order to earn a place on the sideshow platform, each one had to be exceptional and utterly unique. I was less interested in any one of the categories that got them there than in the glue that held them temporarily together. That glue was freakiness, a combination of advertising hype, costuming, and performance that turned the raw material of the body into a sensation people would pay to see. The fact that being a freak was all about drama, a theatrical guise that could be taken on and off at will, distinguished it from more commonplace categories of identity like "disabled," or "black," or "woman."

I appreciated the raw humor of freak shows, which flouted the decorum of respectable society with rude language and off-color jokes. I wrote critically about the woman who sued the New York State Fair for exhibiting Otis Jordan, a man whose arms and legs were braided together by a rare congenital disease. Unable to use his limbs, Otis made the best of his situation by calling himself the Frog Man and showing off his ability to roll cigarettes using only his mouth. Although Otis claimed to love his work, the plaintiff, who had a disability of her own, thought it was degrading. She demanded that the sideshow be banned from the fair. Otis fought back, and the case was defeated. I applauded the court's argument that Otis was entitled to make a living any way he pleased. I accused his detractors of being snobs who clung to musty ideas about politeness and respectability.

Of course, Henry wasn't a freak. But as I tried to figure out what was best for him, it became harder and harder to separate my personal and my academic interests. I found my experiences as a parent increasingly in tension with ideas and beliefs that had been integral to my intellectual landscape. I realized that I was glad Henry had an identity, even if it came from a medical diagnosis. Since he was born, I had met lots of families whose children experienced unexplained developmental delays, catalogues of symptoms that didn't add up to anything particular. They belonged to no group, had nobody to share ideas and resources with, or talk them through difficult moments. The fact that Henry's disability gave him an identity as a person with Down syndrome meant that we had a community of other families who understood us and shared our concerns. As the chronic outsider, I was constantly reminded of how little I had in common with those other parents. There were the vegans and the devoutly religious, people who sold insurance and people who didn't work at all, very rich people, very poor people, people who spoke other languages and people who had never been to college, all held together by little more than a shared diagnosis. But that diagnosis had reshaped our lives. Under the right circumstances, it overshadowed our individual differences. Identity became a magnet that held us together and a guide for how we understood the world. It promised us that we wouldn't have to face the battles and triumphs of raising our children alone.

I also wanted Henry to be included. The freak's flamboyant outsiderness wasn't so appealing when I started to think about what I wished for my own child. I wanted him to have the same opportunities and pleasures as other children. I wanted people to look beyond his difference, not assume that it was a marker of what he could and couldn't

Surprised by Disability

199

do. I was appalled to think that people might stare at him or judge him by his appearance rather than his abilities. As Henry's mother, I was deeply grateful for the activists who had fought to allow people like him to go to school, have jobs, and receive the support they needed to live full and productive lives.

I found myself becoming one of those parents who signed petitions and wrote letters of protest. I still believed that Otis Jordan had the right to exhibit himself, but I could also see why his accuser, who was herself disabled, would find the spectacle painful and humiliating. I bristled at the retard jokes that seemed to crop up like poisoned mushrooms in movies, on TV shows, and in the mouths of politicians. My thrill at seeing Barack Obama elected president was compromised when he laughingly told Jay Leno he bowled like someone in the Special Olympics and when White House chief of staff Rahm Emanuel called a plan to run ads against moderate Democrats "fucking retarded." I stopped a graduate student in the middle of an oral exam because he described something as "retarded." I couldn't do much about the language of politicians or Hollywood comedies, but I could ask a doctoral candidate and future teacher to think carefully about his choice of words.

My friend Rosemarie Garland Thomson, a well-known scholar of disability studies, once remarked on the paradox of disability. If we live long enough, it will happen to all of us. And yet when it happens it always comes as a surprise. Maybe it's almost impossible for an able-bodied person to believe that in the blink of an eye we could find ourselves crippled by illness or accident. Or the more likely scenario that with time and age our bodies will gradually become slower, weaker, and more prone to sickness. Maybe in our heart of hearts we know this all too well and the prospect of becoming disabled is so scary that we shun people with disabilities, as if their impairments were an infectious disease. Our collective repulsion-tinged-with-fear helps to explain the stigma of disability. Much as the able-bodied believe that people with disabilities deserve to be fully included in our society, they may also fervently wish for them to just go away and stop reminding the rest of us of our own vulnerability. This leads to a vicious cycle because the more people with disabilities are shunned and ostracized, the more the able-bodied fear becoming just like them.

Another source of stigma is the association of disability with suffering. For the first time in history, we live in a society that believes it is possible to go through life free of pain. The industries of modern medicine, diet, and fitness are founded on the promise that health is entirely within our control. People with disabilities are proof that this isn't true, that disease and accident can happen to anyone. Even if we're lucky enough to avoid sickness and injury, we all grow older, facing the inevitable infirmities and weaknesses that come along with an aging body. We protect ourselves against this realization by projecting our fears onto the disabled body, as if only people with disabilities endure pain and suffering. In truth, many people with disabilities lead full and satisfying lives. There's lots of research to prove that the disabled are no unhappier than any other segment of the population. And of course many able-bodied people suffer too. It's impossible to live without experiencing pain. If we could somehow accept the truth of Rosemarie's first point, seeing disability, much like aging, as an inevitable part of life, maybe it wouldn't scare us so much. Maybe we would learn to really accept, and not simply to tolerate, the presence of people with disabilities among us. And maybe we could turn our attention to accommodating, rather than trying to eliminate them.

I felt energized by these insights. They gave my work a new sense of purpose. I realized how lucky I was to have a job where I could use my research and teaching to share what I had learned with other people. I decided to plunge right in. A center on campus was offering funds to support collaborative research projects on problems of "social difference." I thought that disability certainly fit the bill. It was the most common form of human difference, and one that was clearly shaped by cultural and environmental factors. I drew up a proposal for a working group and a series of public programs. It was easy for me to interest colleagues at nearby colleges and universities (and even some from farther away who promised to fly in for our meetings), and soon I had a large roster of graduate students and faculty who agreed to become project fellows. A few months later, I was told that my project had been chosen from a large pile of applications. Nobody on our campus had given much thought to disability, and my colleagues thought it would intersect well with other projects sponsored by the center. It was time to start planning.

I decided to hold several meetings to gather ideas from interested colleagues. Although I had written a book about freak shows, I was still testing the waters of disability studies, and I knew I could benefit from the collective wisdom of our group. That was when I realized how much I still had to learn. After I reserved space in the center's seminar room, a colleague in a wheelchair gently pointed out that it was located in one of the most inaccessible parts of the campus. The problems weren't insurmountable, he reassured me, as long as we included careful instructions for wheelchair users. As I read through his directions, I realized how many times I had walked to that building without giving a second thought to how it might be accessed by a person with disabilities. From the street, the wheelchair user had to be escorted by a security guard to an elevator requiring swipe-card access to the upper campus. Once there, she would need to make her way to our building. A ramp would take her inside, where she would catch an elevator to the sixth floor, go down the hall through several sets of heavy doors to the building annex, then take a second set of elevators up to the next level to reach our meeting room. An alternate route, which involved only one elevator, required visitors to use a back entrance located behind a dark, foul-smelling loading dock. Although I was dismayed to realize how challenging it would be for a wheelchair user to get to the meeting, I decided that problems like this were to be expected of a campus built in the nineteenth century. As long as the directions were clear, people could plan their route in advance and we would all end up in the same place.

On the day of the meeting, I was reassured by the number of people who showed up, crowding around the seminar table and filling chairs around the sides of the room. Clearly, these were issues that my group cared about enough to navigate an unwelcoming route. A lively, contentious discussion had started when somebody got a text message from a colleague in a wheelchair who had just been dropped off by her Access-A-Ride service. The van had been infuriatingly late, but she was on her way up. Twenty minutes later, another text came in to report that she was still unable to get to the meeting. Ten minutes after that she wheeled into the room, bristling with rage. She had left her directions at home. After the van dropped her off, the security guard had no idea how to admit her to the building or direct her to an appropriate entrance. It had taken her half an hour of wrong turns, a broken elevator, and unhelpful staff to get to the room. "This is simply unacceptable," she announced breathlessly.

My first reaction was a pang of irritation. She was derailing my meeting, which was off to such a good start. I had gone out of my way to provide detailed directions, and she hadn't used them.

I quickly realized that this was unfair. If I arrived at an unfamiliar university without directions, I would expect that a campus map or security guard would be able to help me find my way. Why should it be any different for a person in a wheelchair? Her troubles weren't a distraction, they were a vivid illustration of why we were there. My project had to address not only the intellectual issues involved in the study of disability but the very real challenges of access that determined whether people with disabilities would be genuinely included in the life of our university.

That was how I became an unwitting, and often bumbling, crusader. It wasn't a full-time job, of course. I still spent the majority of my waking hours figuring out how to get Henry the support he needed to be included at school. When I did make it on campus, most of my time went to figuring out how to make sure my students and colleagues with disabilities had the same. At a panel I organized on disability and the university, the stories we heard were grim. A colleague in a wheelchair told us about going into an underground passage connecting two campus buildings. Once the entrance locked behind him, he discovered that the door at the other end refused to open with his swipe card. Although he is a vigorous man of middle age, the maintenance worker who came to his rescue clapped him on the shoulder and condescendingly called him "pops." A student with a sensory processing disorder needed to sit in the front row of class, taking her notes on a laptop computer. She had a professor who insisted that laptops could be used only in the back of the room. After she explained her situation, he announced to the entire class that he was making a "special exception" for her. A student with multiple sclerosis arrived at the address given for an end-of-the-year party only to find that the restaurant was at the bottom of a dauntingly steep incline, accessible only by foot. Other students reported broken elevators, stairs without handrails, difficulty with sign interpreters.

The news wasn't all bad. One student with muscular dystrophy told us that he had been welcomed into the marching band, and another described her professors as generous and accommodating. A professor who uses a wheelchair and had been around since the 1980s insisted that disability access at our university was much better than it had been in the recent past. The panelists and audience agreed that there was a general climate of acceptance and goodwill toward accommodating people with disabilities on campus.

They also agreed that goodwill was hardly enough. But neither were the requirements for "reasonable" accommodation mandated by the Americans with Disabilities Act. "Reasonable" is a shifty, subjective term, especially when historic architecture, academic rigor, and intellectual integrity are part of the conversation. Although our university was compliant with the law, its efforts clearly were falling far short of creating a genuinely inclusive and barrier-free environment for people with disabilities. The challenges we discussed would only increase with the identification of growing numbers of students with invisible disabilities like autism, bipolar disorder, chronic fatigue syndrome, epilepsy, or stuttering. Their needs were less immediately apparent and often far trickier to accommodate, requiring individual negotiations on a case-by-case basis. Modifications in the classroom did little to mitigate the more subtle ways people with disabilities are told that they're unwelcome on our campus: locating a ramp in a dark loading dock, holding parties and other extracurricular events in inaccessible locations, or offering accommodations only for talks specifically related to the topic of disability.

I had heard stories like these for years. But instead of inspiring me to act, they made me want to run away. Eventually, I stopped writing about disability because I didn't want to be an activist. I loved books and archives, where history came packed away in boxes and binders, but every approach I took inevitably led back to these thorny social and political issues involving real people and their messy problems. That was me in another life. Before. Once I came to see, in a very personal way, the importance and value of including people with disabilities, it was impossible not to want to change my world. I realized my work wasn't just about words on a page. I could use it to do something very real and very important. Learning how to interact with and accommodate students and colleagues with disabilities could benefit us all. It was clear that everyone stood to gain from better campus maps, working elevators, ramps, and hand rails. Anyone with a shopping cart full of library books or a sprained ankle knows that. But accommodating more subtle and less visible disabilities could also make us rethink how we taught, what we valued, and why our work mattered. People with visual impairments raised questions about why I privileged print over oral communication, and the importance I placed on visual images in my teaching; students who needed extra time on their exams made me wonder why I was trying to cram an entire semester's worth of learning into a fifty-minute package dictated by the campus registrar; a young man with manic depression made me reconsider my request that all students speak at least once during each seminar meeting.

At the end of the semester, my colleagues in narrative medicine invited Michael Bérubé to campus to give a talk. I was delighted when they asked me to introduce him. I also wanted him to meet Henry, so I had Angela bring him for a quick visit just before the event started. Everybody cooed over Henry's winning smile, and he ate up the attention. When he clambered out of the stroller and took off across the room, Michael admired how well he got around. When it was time for him to go, Henry waved sweetly and made his best effort at saying "bye bye." Although it was the end of the semester, a large and enthusiastic crowd turned out for the talk. I still couldn't help feeling disappointed that nobody from my parents group showed up. I had advertised it on our email list, thinking it would be a great opportunity to bring my professional and personal lives together. I had learned so much from the world of disability studies that I wanted to share with other families. I also thought the parents I knew had a lot to teach scholars about what it meant to live with disability.

When it was time, I introduced Michael by telling the story of my multiple encounters with *Life as We Know It*, first as a meditation on the philosophical and political challenges raised by disability, and then as a much more personal source of comfort and wisdom. I described how, while I was in the hospital with Henry, Jon had stayed up late reading Michael's book. "Of course we knew that Henry would be an individual with his own personality and abilities—not a clone of Jamie," I explained, "but in the first weeks of our son's life, *Life as We Know It* became our guide, a portrait of what it might mean to have a person with Down syndrome in our family.

"As we struggled to get Henry to drink from a bottle, I would report, 'Michael and Janet had a contest to see who could get Jamie to drink the most milk.'

"Or Jon, who loves geography and maps of all kinds, would say hopefully, 'Do you remember the part where Michael says that Jamie has an incredible sense of direction?'

"Or, as we thought fearfully of how Noah might be affected by having a brother with a disability, we would remember Michael's stories of how Jamie taught his older brother about kindness, compassion, and appreciation for difference.

"As scholars we aspire to write books that will enlighten and inspire our readers. Some of us succeed. But it is the rare literary critic whose books also offer wisdom and comfort in a time of crisis. Michael's book did precisely that for me and my family, and for numerous other parents I've met in the years since Henry was born."

Unlike some introductions I've given, this time I meant every word that I said. I went back to my seat, looking forward to the talk Michael had promised, which would be an update on some of the things Jamie had been doing and thinking in the years since *Life as We Know It* was published. I knew he would tell lots of funny and moving stories, while continuing to remind us of how these personal anecdotes were linked to the larger social and political problems facing people with disabilities in our society.

Michael didn't disappoint. He talked about Jamie's many accomplishments, his participation in the Special Olympics swim team, his love of Renaissance art, how hard he had worked to learn French, and his first try at living in a group home. Jamie is an experienced traveler, and there were some great stories about the trips they had taken together. Michael is no Pollyanna, and it wasn't all rosy. He talked about Jamie's frustrations, especially how hard it was for him to make real friends and to understand how to "hang out" with his older brother.

Just as he started to talk, Sophie slipped into the chair next to me. "Hi," she whispered, squeezing my leg, "sorry I'm late."

"You missed my introduction," I whispered back with a grin. "But I'm so glad you're here!"

And I meant it. I thought that Sophie, with her intense, quizzical approach to the world, would be an especially good audience for the kind of talk Michael was going to give. I remembered how impatient I had been with her just a few weeks before, how she had turned to me with such sincerity and concern to remind me, *I'm still trying to make sense of things.*

Surprised by Disability

I hoped what Michael had to say would factor into the sense she made. I appreciated how much she was ready to listen and learn as she tried to figure out what was best for her son, and her family. And most of all I was just glad she was there, bringing two strands of my life together, meeting in ways I had never imagined.

I was still trying to make sense of things too.

PART THREE

Transition

THE MONTHS BEFORE HENRY TURNED three were a time of endings and goodbyes. In theory, early intervention serves children from birth to age three. But because of Henry's birthday, we were told we had to terminate his services in August, when he would be just over two and a half. In New York, children unlucky enough to be born in December have to exit the program in time to start preschool in September. Although Henry would be staying at the Family Center, he still had to transition to be eligible to move on with the rest of his class.

This news came as something of a surprise, since staff at the Family Center had assured us that Henry could start the preschool room in the fall while keeping his early intervention services until December. That April the school administration abruptly reversed course and informed us we had to begin the preschool evaluation process immediately. We were indignant. Many parents spend months planning the transition by lining up new therapists and getting evaluations, schedules, and paperwork in order. In the past, the Family Center had allowed children with fall birthdays to stay in early intervention, and nobody seemed to think anything was amiss. We wanted to continue our current services until the last possible second, since moving into the Committee on Preschool Special Education (CPSE) would inevitably mean cuts in Henry's program, battles with over-worked bureaucrats, and the loss of Sarah Lee, our wonderfully supportive early intervention coordinator.

I couldn't help obsessing over the arbitrary injustice of birthdays. If Henry had been born only a week later, he would be entitled to six additional months in early intervention. Henry's classmate Francesca, who was just two weeks younger, could stay in early intervention until the following summer simply because she was born in early January. It didn't seem fair to cut him off, especially given how much he stood to gain from the extra support. We made our protest known with phone calls and letters to the Bank Street administration. They apologized for the confusion, but insisted that nothing could be done. The only way Henry could move into Room 3 was to complete his transition by the end of August.

I couldn't help feeling betrayed. The Family Center represented itself as a home away from home, a loving environment where each child was accepted regardless of background or abilities. How could they claim to be a second family while also hewing so closely to the utilitarian demands of the board of education? I became aware of a gulf dividing the teachers, who couldn't have been more nurturing and supportive, from an administration beholden to an impersonal government bureaucracy. When the two were at odds, it was clear who was going to win. This conflict was an important reminder that Henry's place at the Family Center was funded by the state. First early intervention, and then the board of education, would finance the wonderful opportunities for inclusion and learning that the Family Center had to offer, but Henry would attend on their terms, no matter how rigid or arbitrary they might seem to us.

In what felt like a lifetime ago (really the previous fall), I had volunteered to teach summer school. For a full professor, the pay seemed generous, especially since it was a short six-week term. At the time, I imagined the extra money as a buffer against the insecurities of the faltering economy and the unknown expenses of Henry's educational future. But I hadn't thought through the challenges of cramming an entire semester's worth of work into those six weeks. I was already burned out by the exams and grading and meetings that pile up at the end of spring semester. Just as I was trying to get my mind around how I could possibly manage summer school teaching on top of all the research and writing I had already committed myself to doing, the full force of the CPSE transition hit. The board of ed requires all students requesting services under CPSE to undergo an extensive evaluation process. Not only would I need to collect reports from each of Henry's current therapists, but I would also have to schedule observations by specialists in each developmental domain. Their evaluations would have to acknowledge delays significant enough to warrant ongoing services but not so severe as to raise questions about whether he really belonged in an integrated preschool. I would then need to pore over the massive list of approved providers distributed by the board of education to find replacements for each of Henry's current therapists and figure out a new schedule for his many appointments.

Looking back at the worn folders overflowing with Henry's transition materials, I'm struck that, from the moment he emerged from my body, every aspect of my son's abilities and potential has been tracked, evaluated, and assessed. There is something unseemly about the sheer quantity of paper, the hours of work represented by those voluminous reports, and the clear inadequacy of the scores and percentiles it all boils down to. What do those numbers tell about the value of a life? Or even the value of what any given child might bring to his or her classroom? Many of these standardized tests were first designed in the 1920s, when they entered the American educational system as part of the eugenics movement. Although eugenics is more commonly associated with Nazi Germany, it had a long and robust history in the United States. In the 1880s Sir Francis Galton proposed that the human race could be perfected through selective breeding. A proponent of social Darwinism (and the half-cousin of Charles Darwin), he believed that the innate superiority of the upper classes was due to generations of reproduction among the fittest members of the British population. He also came up with the concept of standardized testing, which influenced the French psychologist Alfred Binet's notion of the "intelligence quotient." In my reading, Binet had emerged as an unlikely hero. Skeptical of the prevailing science of craniometry— which sought to correlate intelligence with head size—Binet looked for other strategies for measuring human intelligence. The scale he developed was intended to identify children who required extra educational support, and he advocated for programs tailored to their particular needs and challenges. He objected to the idea that intelligence was merely hereditary, believing that the individual child is shaped by a complex interaction of inheritance and environment. So too, Binet opposed the notion of intelligence as a fixed quantity, recognizing that it could be shaped and nurtured by the right kind of education. When Binet's scale traveled to America, it was put to more specious uses based on the assumption that intelligence was a static, heritable trait belonging to entire groups, rather than individuals. In the United States, the IQ test was applied to whole populations in order to justify a host of nasty prejudices, including anti-miscegenation laws, restrictions on immigration, and enforced sterilization of the poor, criminals, and the disabled.

With some modifications, today we use the same tests that were designed to ferret out weakness and inferiority to determine a child's intellectual potential. While IQ still factors into the detection of intellectual disability, it also plays an important part in identifying students as "gifted." I knew this grim history when we marched four-year-old Noah through three different sets of standardized tests. We knew they measured little more than whether he was good at taking tests. That, and whether his parents and teachers had put him through the battery of expensive practice materials sold by test prep companies promising to give your child an extra edge. We knew it, but refusing to test seemed futile, since we also knew that good scores would give us the best possible chance of finding a kindergarten that was right for him. To our relief, after all the worry and bother he ended up getting in to a school we loved, which didn't use standardized tests in its admission process.

It seemed terribly wrong to be using the same kinds of tests that told us our older son was outstanding in every domain to document our younger son's delays. But there was no other way to get Henry the services he needed. Henry would be evaluated based on his ability to complete a prescribed sequence of activities with only minimal prompting. For the physical therapist, these might include walking in a straight line, throwing a ball, or getting up from a seated position. For the psychologist, it was puzzles and pretend play. The speech therapist tested his receptive and expressive language. The occupational therapist had him stacking blocks and drawing circles. I was allowed to observe but wasn't supposed to intervene. Sometimes I was pleasantly surprised at Henry's ability. Most of the time I was biting my tongue as he failed at basic activities I knew he was perfectly capable of doing. Unlike Noah, who had a powerful desire to succeed at the kinds of challenges presented by a standardized test, Henry seemed not to care at all. In fact, he often seemed deliberately to underperform, as if he resented being asked to do silly things. I appreciated the sense of self that led Henry to resist, while knowing his rebelliousness would probably at times undermine his chances at success.

Everyone came away charmed by Henry. The reports describe him as "a lovely, cheerful, self-assured little boy," "a sweet, adorable, and friendly child," "very related to others," "interested in interacting," and "delightful." In each case, the glowing initial impressions were followed by more detailed, and far less glowing, descriptions of his abilities. One teacher told me that Henry had "scatter skills," a term that describes greatly varied levels of competence across different domains. The unevenness was obvious even within the same test. In speech, his receptive language (ability to understand and act on what he was hearing) was months beyond his expressive language (ability to communicate). The psychologist noted that at thirty-one months, he could do one puzzle at a thirty-three-month level but another at only a nineteen-month level. Somehow, it all added up to a score that placed him in the 5th percentile for his age. After almost three years, I should have been used to it. But the overachiever in me chafed at having a child who was ranked below average in every respect.

The good in having reports like these was that it would be easy to make the case for retaining, and even increasing, the services Henry was already receiving under early intervention. Armed with a thick folder of evaluations and several pages of talking points, Jon and I showed up for our first meeting with the board of ed. After waiting for almost an hour, we were finally ushered into a small, windowless room. Unlike early intervention, where families have a service coordinator to support and advocate for them, in CPSE we were on our own. We had been warned to expect nothing from the rumpled, elderly "parent advocate" who shook our hands gently and then retreated to a seat in the corner, where she dozed for the rest of the meeting. We had also been warned that CPSE runs on an ever-shrinking budget, which can be a rude awakening after the generous resources offered by early intervention. Add to this that CPSE is designed to address a narrowing set of concerns. Where early intervention is about broad support for the child and family, CPSE is focused specifically on education. We would have to argue that the services we were requesting were essential to Henry's future success as a student.

Once we were seated around the table, our CPSE administrator started the meeting with a resigned sigh, before telling us how many days were left until he could retire. In a pleasant enough tone, he informed us that funds were limited, and he would do his utmost to satisfy Henry's minimum needs, while always keeping his best interests in mind, of course. We nodded politely, and I felt my heart beginning to pound as I waited for the moment when we would have to lay out our requests. I had my speech carefully planned. I would start by showing a photo of Henry grinning adorably at the camera, putting a human face on the reams of evaluations spread out on the table. Then I would carefully review his needs in each domain, referring to the evaluations—checkered with colored flags to mark out key passages—for evidence. I planned to conclude by listing the frequency and duration of each of the specific therapies he required.

I waited expectantly, looking for my invitation to speak. It never came. Instead, the administrator peered down at his files as if seeing them for the first time. "Here's what I'm offering you," he said, listing about half of the services we had in mind. "This is the program, effective next Monday," he said. "You can sign here." He pushed the pile of documents across the desk at us.

I was stunned. I had come to the table armed with the weapons I knew best, expert reports, reams of data and evidence, my own carefully scripted eloquence. Nobody seemed interested in hearing what I had to say. I shook my head, feeling a lump in my throat. "That's not what we had in mind," I sputtered. Leaving the picture of Henry in my bag, I launched into an abridged version of my speech. When I finished, the administrator looked at me, unmoved.

"You're asking a lot," he said, noncommittal.

I glanced at Jon, waiting for him to back me up.

Jon is a lawyer and he makes arguments for a living. In the same tone I had heard him use on the phone with difficult clients, he laid out our case, point by point. The administrator looked at him, unmoved.

"Please," Jon said. "We know you have rules. But Henry was born on December 24. Because of his birthday, he's been forced to do everything early. He'll have to go to kindergarten at age four. Please give him this chance to catch up." He was no longer speaking as a lawyer. Henry was our son. And this was a precious moment of opportunity to shape his future.

There was a long pause, while the administrator seemed to consider his options. "Okay," he said with a shrug. He looked at the clock, and I imagined he was thinking about lunch. "I can do that." He started to scribble amendments to the pages in front of him, adding all of the extra services we had requested.

Then his brow furrowed. He looked up at us. "Here's what I don't understand. Why is he at the Family Center? If he needs all these services, wouldn't he be better off in a self-contained class where he could get constant support?"

Transition

My heart sank. I realized we had argued ourselves into a difficult position. We had claimed Henry required more therapy than the administrator was prepared to offer. But we also had to prove he was capable enough to belong in an integrated classroom. If he were in a self-contained program where all of the children were delayed, he might get more specialized attention.

The answer seemed so obvious. "He needs the Family Center precisely because of his delays." I could see exactly where to go with this argument. "He needs a lot of individualized therapy to help with his physical weakness and learning challenges. But he also needs to be surrounded by typical children who can stimulate him and give him models for social development. He wouldn't get that in a self-contained class. Henry is exactly the kind of child who thrives in an integrated setting."

I could see we had won. The administrator, who had just ticked off two more hours toward his retirement, was nodding his approval to our revised program. There would be at least another hour of paper-work, stacks of documents to be approved and signed, long delays while he battled with an aging copy machine. But none of this mattered, because we had secured the education and support Henry needed, and it would be a whole year before we had to fight this battle again.

We walked out into the shimmering heat of a September morning and hailed a cab. In the cool of the air-conditioned backseat, we heaved a collective sigh of relief. "That was harder than I thought it would be," Jon said. "But we won. We did something good for our boy." He put his hand on top of mine.

I nodded. It was all true. I felt a fleeting burst of admiration for Jon, whose intervention seemed to have turned the tables in our favor. But I couldn't help seeing the glass half-empty. At home I had a

T-shirt with Eeyore printed on the front. Jon always commented on how perfectly it fit. I couldn't enjoy our victory without immediately seeing its dark side.

"I'm just worried," I said, pulling my hand away. "I don't know how I'm going to manage this new program. CPSE providers won't come to the apartment, and I'm honestly not sure how Henry can possibly get to so many different appointments every week."

Jon tensed with irritation. "Okay. But can't you take one minute to be happy about what we've done? Why do you always have to go straight to the negative? Why are you turning this into something bad?"

I took the bait. "Because I have to do all the work to make it happen!" I wailed. "Your job is done. On paper, we got Henry everything he needs. But now I have to set it up. I have to find the therapists. I have to make the schedule. I have to figure out how to get him there and back. Sometimes I just feel overwhelmed."

This continued to be one of the most tired arguments in our playbook. Jon worked long, inflexible hours to pay our bills, and I managed the life of our family while trying to squeeze my own work into the time left after everybody else was taken care of. Sometimes it all ran like a well-oiled machine, but transitions always put a kink in the works. I knew this one would be especially challenging to figure out. We sat in silence until the taxi pulled up at the corner where I would get out, while Jon continued on to the office. I slammed the door much harder than necessary, and headed inside. I knew I would spend much of the afternoon on the phone trying to arrange our new schedule. When that was done, I would have to plan the next day's summer school class, walk the ten blocks to pick Noah up from BT, and feed, bathe, and put both children to bed before turning to the assigned reading that would take me well into the night.

Later, there would be apologies on both sides. Jon would tell me that he appreciated how much I did for Henry. I would be sorry for spreading gloom over our moment of victory, and for making Jon feel guilty about having to work so hard. But I couldn't help feeling that this was a conflict we would never fully resolve. No matter how good his intentions, Jon simply didn't have a life where he could be closely involved in scheduling and maintaining Henry's daily activities. And no matter how much I wanted to be at the center of the action, I knew I would never completely escape feeling oppressed by the constant, competing demands on my time.

As it turned out, getting Henry moved into his CPSE services would be incredibly demanding. The transition can be relatively painless if your therapists work under both early intervention and CPSE. None of ours did. This meant that Henry would have a complete turnover in his services. Where early intervention had provided us with a coordinator to make sure everything was running smoothly, CPSE left us to our own devices. After a seemingly endless string of emails, phone calls, and interviews, I was finally able to assemble a team of therapists who worked on the Upper West Side and accepted CPSE.

It would be another herculean task to fit all of them into Henry's schedule. Unlike early intervention, where one session can be lined up directly after another, I now had to consider the transportation time involved in getting Henry from one therapist's studio to the next. Each had only a few openings a day, and trying to reconcile them with the times Henry was available was like trying to solve a Rubik's cube. No sooner did I get one set of appointments lined up than another popped out of place. Even when everybody's regular times were set, it seemed there was always someone who wanted to change or cancel. The weekly schedule was so complicated that I would write it on a dry-erase board hanging in our kitchen and make a printout for Angela to take along to remind her where Henry had to be each afternoon. As soon as his day at the Family Center ended, Angela would hurry him from one appointment to another, sometimes as many as three in a single afternoon.

Hard as it was, we were ready for this transition. Where once Henry had worked compliantly in any setting, he had started to resist being told what to do in his own home. At the end of a long day, he didn't want a physical therapist showing up to make him climb stairs or balance on his hands. He didn't want to have a speech and language pathologist managing how he ate his snack or an occupational therapist greeting him first thing in the morning to make him string beads and do puzzles. One day he sobbed melodramatically throughout an entire session of occupational therapy. As soon as the clock ran out and the therapist gave me the paperwork to sign, the tears stopped immediately. It was clearly time for Henry to move on. Much as I hated transitions, truth be told, I was ready to stop being so involved in Henry's therapy as well. Participation meant different things with different therapists. Some wanted me to help by distracting Henry. Some wanted everyone cleared out of the room so that Henry's attention was focused on what they were doing. And some let me just observe. But all of it added up to many hours a week when I wasn't able to work or take care of other parts of our life. I would miss being included on a daily basis, but I could also think of many productive ways to use the extra time.

I liked Henry's new CPSE providers well enough, but I wouldn't form the same intimate relationships with them as I had with the early intervention therapists. I tried to keep up with Henry's progress by taking him to his appointments when I had time off. The therapists always welcomed me, and were happy to explain what they had been working on. When I visited their studios, I realized that Henry was starting to have a life of his own, and he had formed a close relationship with each therapist. With Laura, his occupational therapist, a blue stuffed bear was his favorite toy. He always got himself a drink of water before starting a session of physical therapy with Sheila. Maryanne, his speech therapist, taught him to pull his own pants down when he went to the bathroom. I was gratified to see how much Henry's new therapists loved him and appreciated his progress. At the same time, it made me sad to discover that he was already beginning to inhabit a world that didn't include me. Much as I wanted Henry to be independent, it was hard to let go of my desire to control and be involved in every aspect of his life.

The transition to CPSE wasn't just about new beginnings; it was about saying goodbye to Henry's old team, too. Some of Henry's therapists had been with us since he was born. All of them had spent hours in our home. They had held Henry while he cried, applauded his accomplishments, and witnessed the chaos and clutter of our daily lives. It was hard to accept that they would be moving on. While they had been such a memorable part of our lives, we were just one of many families that would pass through theirs. In the fall, they would take on new clients, therapy altering the course of their lives just as it had ours.

As usual, the prospect of separation brought out my urgent desire to leave a mark. I couldn't bear the thought of being forgotten, or even blending into a crowd of families past. I needed to stand out from all the other moms who fought and worried and struggled to get their kids what they needed in this life. Of course I baked. For weeks, our kitchen was filled with trays and sheet pans. Every inch of the freezer was packed with dough in various stages of preparation. There were jams and custards and icings to apply. Each therapist would get a large box of cookies and cake. But I wanted them to have something more enduring. I made books filled with pictures of Henry at each stage of life, including some of him working with each therapist. I knew that even if they remembered us, Henry would very quickly forget about them. Except that the hard work they had done with him would be a foundation for all future accomplishments. He would run and jump because Joy, our physical therapist, had taught him to sit up and crawl. He would sit at a desk and write because our first occupational therapists had worked on his grip and his upper body strength. He would eat pizza at a birthday party because of feeding therapists who broke Cheerios into tiny pieces and taught him how to chew. I remembered Jackie doing tracking exercises with balloons and flashcards during her first sessions with Henry. Somehow these would become a platform for Henry to speak words and, eventually, sentences. All the puzzles and games that Alison played with Henry would be a foundation so that one day he would know how to take care of himself, make friends, and succeed at school.

All of this had to do with muscle memory. There is only so much the conscious mind can recall. Not so with muscles. Our muscles are archives that carry the traces of all the actions that have come before, particularly the ones we repeat thousands of times until they become completely habituated, ingrained into the very fiber of our bodies. Most of us don't have to think before we chew, or tie a shoe, or walk up a flight of stairs. We are freed to think about other things because our muscles know what to do. "My muscles will remember you," was the way I ended each therapist's book. What better way to express gratitude for the foundations they had laid?

Always Something

"IT JUST GOES TO SHOW YA: it's always something," Roseanne Rosannadanna, the irrepressible character played by Gilda Radner on *Saturday Night Live*, used to say. I had adopted this as my own inelegant motto.

I couldn't think of any better way to say it. No sooner did I carve out a perfectly empty day to write than somebody got sick. No sooner did he recover than Angela got sick, or a leak in our apartment forced us to flee to a hotel overnight, or Jon got sent to Miami on a few hours' notice, and so on in an endless chain of small calamities, each threatening to derail the elaborate tightrope walk between my work and the life of our family.

I knew there was nothing special about this scenario. Every working parent will immediately understand the precarious balancing act I'm describing. It's just that some of us have better safety nets than others. We happened to have virtually none. And our challenges were multiplied by our struggles with schools and government agencies, and the need to manage Henry's doctors, caregivers, therapists, teachers, and complicated schedule.

Given all of this, I had no right to be surprised by the results of the routine blood test given to Henry on his third birthday. Our pediatrician, Dr. Zimmerman, had been conscientious about drawing Henry's blood every six months, since people with Down syndrome are prone to developing thyroid problems. So far, his thyroid had been doing great.

This time, his thyroid was still fine, Dr. Zimmerman reported. But the lab results showed antibodies associated with celiac disease. I knew something about celiac. Annie, a girl in Noah's preschool class, had been tested the year before, after her parents became concerned that she wasn't growing. When the results came back positive, the doctors told Annie's parents she had celiac, and would need to eliminate all traces of gluten from her diet. Elaborate measures were taken to be sure that her food was gluten-free. Signs and labels cropped up around the preschool warning teachers about what Annie could and couldn't eat, marking her condiments, utensils, and snacks. She also had to avoid contact with ordinary things like Play-Doh, bubbles, and starch, all of which had gluten in them. I saw the stress all of this caused Annie's family, especially her mother, who carried most of the burden of learning about celiac, dealing with doctors, and getting Annie gluten-free. It had been a strain, she admitted, before reassuring me that eventually the diet would become second nature, as it had in her family. I found that hard to believe, feeling unprepared to manage yet another problem.

It turned out that one of the foremost centers for research and treatment of celiac was located at the hospital where Henry was born and where we often saw specialists of one kind or another. Our doctor there explained that celiac is an autoimmune disorder that damages the small intestine, making it unable to absorb nutrients. It's triggered by a reaction to gluten, which is found in wheat, barley, and rye.

There are a whole host of nasty GI symptoms that can give it away. But aside from being on the small side, which was normal for a boy with Down syndrome, Henry had none of them. I learned that celiac can also be invisible, with no sign of the mischief going on inside. It could be years before the more serious consequences emerged, things like other autoimmune disorders, cancers, bone and liver disease, and infertility. The doctor told us that celiac could be confirmed only through a biopsy of the small intestine. Where blood tests could be unreliable, the biopsy was for sure, the gold standard of celiac detection. But it also came with certain risks, since it was a surgical procedure requiring general anesthesia. In Henry's case, the extremely high levels of antibody in his blood combined with Down syndrome made the diagnosis of celiac almost a sure thing, even without the biopsy. Given the circumstances, we could assume that Henry had celiac and put him directly onto the gluten-free diet. "What you can't do," she told us firmly, "is to ignore this. Celiac is dangerous and you need to take it seriously."

Given her certainty, Jon and I saw no reason to put Henry through the unnecessary risk of general anesthesia. A gluten-free diet seemed like the obvious choice. Sure, it would be a nuisance, but how hard could it be?

That was before I understood the meaning of a truly gluten-free diet. Even after seeing how complicated it was to feed Annie, I didn't really get it. I knew foods like bread, pizza, pasta, and cookies contained gluten. What I didn't realize was how many other places it can hide out: bouillon, soy sauce, caramel coloring, beer, oatmeal, Rice Krispies, lunch meats, soups, salad dressings, ordinary pain- and fever-reducing medicines—the list went on and on. Not only did gluten lurk in seemingly innocent foods, but there was the related problem of cross-contamination. Doctors are still trying to figure out how much gluten is enough to cause damage. Some suspect it can be as small as a crumb of bread or even a speck of flour. In order to be on the safe side, a gluten-free food is considered contaminated if it touches anything that has come into contact with gluten. This meant we couldn't use our waffle iron, toaster, cutting boards, colanders, pots, or pans to prepare Henry's food. If we took a scoop of peanut butter, spread it on bread, and dipped the knife back into the jar, the whole container was contaminated. If Henry got Play-Doh under his fingernails, then stuck his hand in his mouth, more contamination. If I baked cookies and a cloud of flour puffed out of the bag, the kitchen had to be scrubbed down. If we made regular pancakes on a griddle, we couldn't use the same surface to cook a gluten-free batch for Henry. The obvious solution was to ban gluten from our household. But the doctors advised against that strategy on the principle that Henry would need to learn how to live in a world filled with gluten. There was no sense in making our home an insulated bubble, or depriving other members of the family. So the rest of us continued to eat gluten. But still, our diet, all of our habits, the organization and cleaning of our kitchen had been turned upside down.

Things were tricky at home, but eating out seemed impossible. You never knew what dangers awaited in the kitchen. French fries were gluten-free, but only if the oil hadn't also cooked onion rings or donuts or breaded chicken or anything else in a batter. Apparently many restaurants added flour to their eggs to make them fluffier. They put slices of bread in the sugar to soak up moisture. Gluten could not be eliminated through high cooking temperatures. That meant pans, grills, and griddles that had touched bread or breaded items couldn't be used to prepare Henry's food. If a restaurant listed gluten-free spaghetti on its menu, we had to be sure it was cooked in a pot that had never held regular pasta. We could order gluten-free pizza only if it wasn't baked on the same surface as the regular pizza. The ingredients in salad dressings, sauces, and condiments all had to be scrutinized. The part of eating in a restaurant that's all about skipping the effort and stress of cooking at home was completely lost. We couldn't go anywhere without packing a cooler of food in case there was nothing on the menu for Henry to eat.

AS THE DRAMA OF HENRY'S celiac was unfolding, I was dealing with dramas of my own. My forty-second birthday was looming. This was a huge milestone. My mother died when she was forty-two. If I could make it through the year, I would have outlived her. I knew I should devote this birthday to celebrating life. But it was hard when my mind filled with thoughts of illness and death. Even though Ruth's journals were buried under a pile of sweaters in my closet, the sense of being haunted was back. As I walked down the street, I felt every intake of breath. I was aware of every minute I lived free of pain. When I tried to write or sit in a meeting I would be distracted by awareness of the hidden interior of my body. What deadly growths might be metastasizing inside me at that very moment? I couldn't seem to summon up the sense of acceptance I had found the previous summer. Instead, I felt a vaguely malevolent, mocking Ruth watching me as I went about my daily life, especially when my kids were around.

At the end of August I had my annual physical. According to my doctor, I was in perfect health. It had become my yearly ritual to ask her about lung cancer. Just to be sure. Was there any chance it was hereditary? Any new research I didn't yet know about? Every year she said there was only the slightest possible genetic connection. Was there anything more to be done? I asked her as usual.

Usually she told me to avoid smoking, just like everybody else. And be sure to get enough exercise. Otherwise, there was nothing.

This time was different. She offered me a lung scan. "If it's really bothering you to the point where it interferes with your life, you can get tested. You need to understand that I'm not recommending it, but if it will make you feel better I can write you a prescription."

I couldn't help wondering whether she suspected something was wrong with me. Did she think I might have cancer? Was that why she was offering me this test, when she never had before?

She insisted there was no reason for the scan other than to relieve my anxiety. "There's also some risk involved. If you get a false positive, that would require more invasive and potentially harmful testing, when in fact you're otherwise healthy. You do have to take that into account in making this decision."

I understood it wasn't a decision to be made lightly. I didn't make any choices right then and there, but I took the prescription. When I got home, I filed it away, an amulet to ward off all that was unknown and uncontrollable about my body and my future.

The easiest thing to do was nothing. I made a decision of a sort by choosing not to decide, and the slip of paper stayed in my desk drawer. I took it out occasionally, just to reassure myself that it was still there. But I made no effort to arrange for a scan, or even to think further about whether it was a good idea. That is, until a few weeks later, when I had dinner with my friend Elizabeth. Very quickly, the conversation turned grim. Her dear friend had just been diagnosed with lung cancer after going to the doctor with a persistent cough, thinking it might be bronchitis or pneumonia. Elizabeth had been with her when she got the news. It had been especially painful because Elizabeth's mother had died suddenly about a year before, and her husband had died of lung cancer not long before that. It was hard to be surrounded by so much sickness and death, and she was struggling to figure out how to talk about it with her son, who was Noah's age.

She thought I might understand especially well, given that I had experienced losses of my own.

At some point during the evening, I told her about the prescription.

"Why wouldn't you get tested?" she asked. Since losing her husband, Elizabeth thought a lot about her own mortality. She didn't want her son to grow up an orphan. "If I were you, I would take the test. Then you don't have to worry. I would do it every few years, just to be sure. Like a mammogram." Suddenly the table felt crowded. Ruth was there, along with Elizabeth's husband and her mom. All watching me expectantly. I could see her point. The scan was a way to avoid becoming like them. I left the restaurant determined to make an appointment the next morning. There seemed no reason not to do it.

That is, until I got home and Jon reminded me of my tendency to develop the symptoms of whatever disease I've been thinking about most recently. He reminded me of the time I was positive I had ringworm. Another time, it was a fatal cyst. Besides that, he was strongly opposed to unnecessary medical procedures. The doctor had pronounced me perfectly healthy. Why go looking for trouble? What if I got a false positive? What if something went wrong?

I didn't know what to do. Both Jon and Elizabeth seemed right. I called my doctor to get her advice. I told her I was thinking about doing the CT scan. If it came back negative, I would be reassured. Then I would do it again in a few years. Being scanned every so often would keep me safe from a stealthy, slow-growing cancer, the kind that discloses itself only when it's too late and your body is already riddled with disease.

"That's not how it works," she told me firmly. "You can't do this kind of scan every two years. This isn't like a mammogram. A CT scan involves exposure to significant levels of radiation. At some point it becomes dangerous. You can do it once, for peace of mind. But I won't prescribe it again."

My heart sank. If I could do the scan only once, that changed everything. What good would it do to take the test once? Even if it told me I was healthy, the next day a cancer might start to grow and I wouldn't know about it. There would be no more scans. As my birthday got closer, I went into a tailspin of fear and anxiety.

One night, Jon and I went out to dinner at a new restaurant. We were fans of the chef, and wanted to get in before the restaurant was reviewed in the *New York Times* and became impossibly crowded. The space was pleasant and inviting, but my food was disappointing. I had had a few glasses of wine by the time the host came over to ask how everything was. Ordinarily, I'm not the kind of person who makes a fuss in restaurants, even if I'm unhappy. But for some reason, I felt compelled to speak up. I gestured at the drab pile of food on my plate: "This lamb is dull, and it looks so unattractive."

I was teaching a class on food, and we had been talking about the tremendous environmental costs of raising meat. It hadn't turned me into a vegetarian, but I had decided to make sure the meat I bought was farmed in an ethical way, even if it was more expensive. I had been moved by the last chapter of Michael Pollan's *The Omnivore's Dilemma*, where he invites his friends to enjoy a meal he hunted and gathered himself. Although it may not have been the best dinner he ever cooked, Pollan concludes, the meal was memorable for being prepared and eaten in a way that honored the food and where it came from. All of this was in my mind as I stared at the spongy, pallid meat in front of me. The host asked me what was wrong with it, his brow furrowing in concern.

"Look at this," I said, gesturing at the plate. I could feel the wine going to my head. "Everything is pale. The meat is beige, and so are the chickpeas, and so is the sauce. There are no colors here, no texture. And it tastes boring. This meal doesn't honor the lamb. I want to do justice to the meat I'm eating." He seemed confused. I could tell he didn't understand. And Jon was looking at me in embarrassment, as if he had no idea what I was trying to say either. The host quickly offered to take the lamb off our bill, and seemed relieved to extricate himself from the conversation.

On the way home, Jon told me I hadn't made any sense. "That guy was really confused when you said you wanted to honor the lamb," he laughed. "What on earth were you talking about?"

"I'm not sure," I confessed. I had felt the need to speak so urgently, but as soon as I opened my mouth I became confused. Even later I couldn't make sense of why it had seemed so important to say something. What I did know with certainty was that there was a lesson for me in that plate, which seemed as rich in metaphorical significance as it was lacking in flavor. Maybe I was the lamb? It had been raised for meat and, like all things, it had to die. At bottom, we humans are meat just like the lamb on my plate. Mind, spirit, soul, essence, are all anchored in the earthy, timebound realities of a fleshly body. Death is inevitable.

But the lamb didn't have to live a miserable life. And it didn't have to come to such a sad end. Maybe I saw myself in that lamb and I was trying to say, in my own confused way, that if I lived a memorable life I hoped I might be honored like a good meal. Or maybe I wanted people to honor whatever life I had managed to live. Could I have identified some message in the way the lamb was prepared and eaten? Isn't the meal we cook from its flesh our way of making sense of a life? We can consume that food quickly and thoughtlessly, or we can take time to think about where it comes from, to transform it into something delicious, and to savor the flavor and nutrients it has to offer. Maybe the lesson was that I needed to do more savoring and less gulping. I had no way of knowing when my life would end, or how. But for the time being I was alive. I could use my life to do good and lasting things, and I hoped they would stay with people like the memory of a meal prepared with love and intention, eaten in good company.

At the time, I really believed some of this. In speaking up, I thought I might have done something to acknowledge the lamb on my plate, and to register my wish that its death had led to something richer and more memorable. Whatever I was trying to say, that tepid, boring dish brought me a level of insight that hadn't been there before. Not just about the way I ate, but about the way I would approach my life. There was nothing to be gained by doing the lung scan. As soon as I got the results, I would start to worry about all the other things I couldn't control or know. But I could do more to appreciate the life I was living now, and try to be in the present rather than always worrying about some future calamity. The prescription was still there in my drawer, but I resolved to put it out of my mind for good.

IF I WERE A DIFFERENT PERSON, our story might end right here. But I'm Eeyore. I see the clouds, not the silver linings. Acceptance is not my natural resting state. The idea that I would conduct my life with intention and balance was all fine and good. But it didn't last. I never got the lung scan, but that doesn't mean I went about my daily life filled with equanimity.

Whatever coping strategies I had managed around the coming and going of my forty-second birthday were gone by the time Henry turned three in late December. We learned about his celiac diagnosis just a few weeks before his birthday party. We had rented out a gym in our neighborhood and invited his whole class to come play. I was determined that Henry would eat pizza just like his friends, so I brought along his gluten-free version wrapped in foil. He didn't seem to notice the changes in his diet and liked pizza with rice crust just as well as the traditional kind. More important was the cake. I had been planning it for months. Henry was in love with *Sesame Street*, and I had decided to use brightly colored frosting with Big Bird, Cookie Monster, Grover, and Elmo figurines dancing on top.

The nutritionist at the Celiac Center discouraged my baking project. "I'm not saying it can't be done. You can bake almost anything without gluten," she explained. "But you need to know what you're doing. This doesn't seem like a good time to be experimenting. Besides, there are so many great gluten-free cakes you can buy these days. Why go to all the trouble?"

She had no idea who she was talking to. I would go to my grave before celebrating my son's birthday with a store-bought cake.

After some research, I found a recipe for a vanilla cake that called for a mixture of brown rice, tapioca, and potato flour. I bought new pans in order to avoid cross-contamination. I scrubbed down the kitchen to be sure there was no stray wheat flour in evidence. I made sure I had a fresh bag of sugar and gluten-free vanilla. I imagined a gluten-free cake would be on the dry side, so I decided to douse each layer with a sugary simple syrup before spreading it with jam. Thankfully, there was no gluten in my usual buttercream frosting.

The finished cake was beautiful. There were four layers, coated in a cheery yellow frosting. On top, I piped pictures of Cookie Monster and Elmo, along with the words HAPPY BIRTHDAY HENRY! The figurines danced around the edges. When I picked it up to put it in the refrigerator, it was surprisingly heavy.

The party went well. Henry's friends looked like they were enjoying themselves, and the staff at the gym did most of the work, allowing us to mingle with the other parents. Henry ate his gluten-free pizza happily, and he loved the singing, clapping and laughing uproariously when the cake was put down in front of him. Then it was time to serve it. Carrying the cake back to the kitchen, I was again surprised by its weight. When we cut it open, I learned that gluten-free cakes are not dry. They tend to be overly moist. Without gluten to produce a light, airy crumb, the flours had compressed into a compact mass. The added syrup had turned the whole thing into a sodden sponge with jam spread stickily between the layers. Extra liquid oozed out the bottom. No wonder it had felt like I was carrying an oversized block of cement. Unappetizing as it was, there was nothing to do but serve it anyway. The children were waiting eagerly for the cake that had looked so appealing from the outside. I watched as one child after another took a bite and left the rest on their plates. A few spit it out before dashing off to play. My heart sank. Was this cake another metaphor? Would Henry's diet be yet another way he was different from everybody else? Pizza and birthday cake were the staples of every kid's birthday party we had ever been to. And now he was denied that. I saw parent after parent shake her head as slices of cake were passed around. I couldn't help but see it as a rejection of me or, even worse, of Henry. There was so much left. I was near tears as I imagined dumping the damp, jammy mess into the garbage.

I felt Henry tugging on my sleeve. The other kids had left the table, but he was still sitting happily in his chair. His plate was empty and his face was smeared with jam and icing. "Mommy," he said, as if it were the most wondrous word he had ever spoken. He gestured at the plate in front of him. "More cake."

I nodded distractedly, watching the party organizers clear the plates of uneaten cake from the table.

"More cake," Henry said again, clear as a bell.

Suddenly I realized what he was saying. He liked my cake. And he wanted another piece. But more important, he was asking for it. He was speaking, making a clear request. And I could understand him and give him what he needed. These were the building blocks of future conversations where we would ask questions of each other, give answers, maybe argue or debate. What mattered was that he was talking in words, and I knew what he was saying. This was the foundation of language shared not just between us, but with the rest of the world. My son had found his voice. Henry was beaming at me, as proud of his own utterance as he was delighted by the prospect of more cake.

It was impossible not to smile back as I turned to cut him another slice.

Epilogue

"Mom."

I refuse to stir from the deep, velvety sleep of early morning.

"Mom." The voice at my ear is soft and insistent. I feel fingers stroking my arm. Kisses brush my cheek. I open one eye, determined not to come fully awake.

It's still dark and Henry is standing by my side of the bed, clearly ready to start his day. We've tried every trick in the book, with little success at breaking his habit of painfully early rising.

"IPad?" he asks softly, hopefully. Like every other kid we know, Henry has become an addict, understanding intuitively how to manipulate the screen, moving effortlessly from one app to another. He likes YouTube best because he can watch clips of *The Muppets*, his favorite show. At first we were mystified by Henry's love for *The Muppets*. Aside from the fact that some of the characters are puppets, the show seemed so talky and adult. We soon realized that even if he isn't getting all the words, Henry can understand the social dynamics behind them perfectly well. He laughs uproariously at Miss Piggy's constant, failed pursuit of Kermit, Animal's id-driven outbursts, the Swedish chef's inscrutable jabbering, the grumpy exchanges between Statler and Waldorf. The Muppets haven't always been the best role models. When he gets restless, Henry likes to sweep piles of papers and books onto the floor with a Miss Piggy–style karate chop or rage through the apartment like Animal. But mostly we're charmed by Henry's passion, and we enable it by playing him songs from the show and listening to his endless renditions of favorite skits.

"Mommy. I want iPad," he says softly. "YouTube?"

My eyes are now fully open. Part of me is furious at having my sleep disturbed. Another part knows I'll be glad if I get out of bed. I love the calm quiet of the very early morning before we begin the frantic race to get everyone out of the apartment on time.

I get up and take Henry's hand, leading him firmly toward the bathroom as he tries to veer off for the living room, where we keep the iPad. While he pees, I toy with the idea of going back to sleep. But by the time we've washed our hands, I'm wide awake too. Suddenly I'm hit by a wave of inspiration. Instead of handing Henry the iPad and going back to bed, I decide we'll work on his literacy program.

"Do you want to do reading?" I say in the most enthusiastic voice I can muster at 5:45 A.M.

"No," he says, chin down, suddenly sullen.

"With mommy on the couch?" I bubble. "Come on. Let's try it."

"No." He crosses his arms firmly.

"Okay, Henry," I tell him. "First reading, then iPad." Henry responds well to sequences. As with most of us, he's much more likely to do something hard or unpleasant if he knows a reward is coming. But this trick doesn't always work. The bathroom is starting to feel cold, and I'm tempted to give up.

Epilogue

"Okay," he says agreeably. I'm relieved that my plan seems to be working.

We sit on the couch and I take out our literacy folder. Henry started a reading program a few weeks before. He was assigned a tutor who will see him once a week, and we've signed a parental contract pledging to reinforce her efforts with daily practice in between sessions. Henry likes his tutor, who is young and creative about coming up with ways to get him to pay attention. But he doesn't like to work with me, and I'm trying not to turn reading into a struggle.

The program begins with a family book. On each page the phrase "I love" is paired with a simple noun like "Mommy," "Daddy," or "Noah." Henry loves seeing the pictures of our family and has picked up the words quickly. All except for the first page, which is giving us trouble. There, a picture of Henry sits above the words "I am Henry." Henry is certainly not a careful reader, and he has trouble noticing that "am" is different from "love." I decide we'll start at the beginning, tackling the problem of the first page before moving on to the easier parts of the book.

The reading program involves a series of matching and identifying exercises that teach children to recognize individual words and phrases before turning to a book (often homemade, to focus on a child's particular interest or curiosity) that puts them all together. This morning Henry is more patient than usual, and he endures several of the preliminary exercises before sweeping them to the floor and reaching for his book. "No more paper," he says firmly. "Read book."

"Okay, you win," I tell him. "Let's read the book. You read me the book."

He turns to the first page and points to a picture of him wearing funny glasses, a huge grin on his face. "I love Henry."

Epilogue

243

"No, look again," I tell him. "What do the words say?" I point at each word.

"I love Henry." He's staring out the window, not even looking at the page.

"Look, Henry," I say, trying my best to be as patient as the literacy tutor. I hold up flash cards with the words "am" and "love." "These are different. This says 'am.' This one says 'love.' What does this say?" I point to "am."

"I love Henry," he says, grinning up at me. It's hard to tell whether he's really confused or just fooling around.

I sigh with irritation. I haven't even had coffee yet and am ready to give up. What do I know about literacy? My own students arrive ready-made, so precocious and bright, as if they emerged from the womb trained to read Michel Foucault. I'm tempted to pack everything away, but I know if I give in and let the lesson come to an end, Henry will think he can use silliness to get out of it next time.

I go into the kitchen to get a glass of water, walking slowly back to the living room. The apartment is still dark, with the blue light of early morning coming in the windows. I pause in the doorway. Henry has picked up the book and is reading to himself. He points to the cover. "I am Henry," he says as clear as day. He turns the page. "I love Mommy." The next page. "I love Daddy."

"Henry!" I shout. "You're reading the book!" I feel a rush of love and admiration, swooping down to cover him in kisses, mussing the fuzz of his short hair. I know we have a long way to go. I know Henry has a tendency toward silliness, that he relies on charm to weasel out of difficult tasks. I know "I am Henry" isn't exactly "Call me Ishmael." But we all have to start somewhere. I have to marvel at what I'm seeing. My four-year-old son is reading.

Epilogue

Publishing a book takes a long time, and it's almost two years since our story ended. I can't honestly say from that day forward Henry went on to read one increasingly challenging book after another, progressing smoothly along a path toward literary enlightenment. I can't even say that the next time Henry picked up that book, he paid attention to the difference between "am" and "love." This was no Helen Keller–at–the–water pump moment. Henry learns in fits and starts, mastering tasks in his own time and on his terms. We fully expect him to reach the same milestones as his brother, but to do so unevenly, and at his own pace. So far, we haven't been disappointed.

Henry's third birthday seemed like an obvious place to close our story. As his graduation from the early intervention program ushered him into a new bureaucratic identity within the Committee on Preschool Special Education, a chapter in our life came to a close. Under the new system, we were lucky to find therapists as talented and dedicated as the ones who worked with him as a baby. Despite our worries, the board of ed has consistently offered Henry the services he needs. Henry is almost five and he still loves puppets, music, and wrestling. He still has a great sense of humor and a loud, infectious laugh. I've left behind many of the worries that used to keep me awake at night. I no longer worry that Henry won't be able to talk. We don't always understand what he's saying, and the more abstract the sentence the more garbled it sounds. But Henry's speech gets clearer every day. He is so eager to talk that he and Noah have entered a new stage of sibling rivalry, where each tries to express himself loudly enough to drown out his brother. Even celiac has been assimilated into our lives. We have a small list of kid-friendly gluten-free restaurants and a familiar rotation of meals at home.

Epilogue

Of course, new worries have taken the place of the old, and these seem much bigger and harder to resolve. Where will Henry go to school next year? Independent schools are expensive, and few of them want a child like Henry. The alternative is the public schools, which don't seem capable of offering Henry what he needs. We know he'll learn best in a small classroom where teaching is tailored to accommodate children with many different abilities. Will Henry have friends? He's always well liked by his peers because he is so funny and agreeable. But he's also hard to understand and doesn't yet know how to play with children of his own age. He seems to like everyone equally well, which also means that he doesn't single anybody out in the way Noah does when he decides somebody is destined to be his friend. And then there are the more distant worries about Henry's adult future, how independent he will be, where he will live, whether he will find meaningful work and relationships. I just try to repress those.

It's hard to believe that just five years ago a hospital social worker told me there were no support groups for families of people with Down syndrome. Since then, so much has changed in our local community. There is a growing network of support systems, and better efforts to reach out to new and expecting parents. One group of families started the Romp for Research, an annual fund-raiser for the Down Syndrome Research and Treatment Foundation, which focuses on studying cognitive and physiological concerns. Another parent organized our chaotic email exchanges into a listserv that now reaches well over a hundred people, who share resources, announcements, and advice. Another started a monthly support group for families in Manhattan and the Bronx. In early 2012 a chapter of GiGi's Playhouse Down Syndrome Awareness Center opened in Harlem. It offers opportunities to socialize and share information, as well as free classes and tutoring. It also sponsors the literacy program that is teaching Henry to read, and there are plans to add math and handwriting support, all free of charge. Because I know how important GiGi's will be for Henry's future, I joined the board and became coordinator of adult programming. After working all day and putting my children to bed, the last thing I want to do is to plan events for GiGi's, and in those bleary late-night hours I often curse my need to stick my nose into every opportunity that comes along. But GiGi's is so new and its success relies completely on the efforts of individual parents. Since our family doesn't have a lot of money to contribute, I try to give my time and energy instead.

The changes I've seen aren't just local. Since Henry was born, Down syndrome has an increasingly public face in movies like the Spanish *Yo También* (*Me Too*), starring Pablo Pineda, the documentary *Monica and David*, and *Girlfriend*, starring Evan Sneider. Lauren Potter continues to appear on the TV show *Glee*, where the character of Sue Sylvester (whose late sister had Down syndrome) just gave birth to a baby with Down syndrome. I continue to fill Henry's scrapbook with stories of success and inclusion: a teenager with Down syndrome who competes on the high school swim team, a couple with Down syndrome (she) and cerebral palsy (he) who live independently in their own apartment, a drummer with Down syndrome who plays with the band Flame. Given the less-than-accommodating world these teenagers and adults were born into, I have to appreciate their accomplishments. I also believe there must be ways to affirm the value of people with Down syndrome that don't rely on trotting out the same list of exceptionally able and successful individuals time and time again. People with Down syndrome who aren't rock stars or athletes or award-winning actors are equally deserving of opportunities to lead full, satisfying, and dignified lives.

Epilogue

There is progress in the realm of science. In the summer of 2011, the *New York Times Magazine* published a story about the neuroscientist Dr. Alberto Costa, who is researching drugs to improve cognition in people with Down syndrome. His work is promising, but I found it all the more hopeful to see Down syndrome featured in such a widely read and respected publication. The following year I heard a presentation by Dr. Todd Kinsella, who reported that the pharmaceutical company Roche is also in the early stages of developing another set of drugs to enhance the cognition, memory, and adaptive behaviors of people with Down syndrome. Other researchers are working on the connection with Alzheimer's and dementia, which tend to strike a disproportionate number of adults with Down syndrome at a relatively young age. I'm struck by how many of these developments have happened in the five years since Henry was born, and hopeful that the next decades will see continued improvement in the care and treatment of people with Down syndrome.

At the same time, I'm well aware that the very idea of a drug to treat the effects of Down syndrome goes against the core beliefs of many scholars and activists of disability. Scientific research is premised on trying to correct the deficiencies and limitations of people with Down syndrome. It focuses on their slow pace of learning, trouble retaining information, and limited adaptive functions, asking whether there are ways to improve the ways their brains are wired. While the scientists don't quite describe Down syndrome as a disease, their work is always framed in terms of correction, improvement, or compensation. By contrast, disability studies emphasizes the social environment, rather than flaws or inadequacies in the individual. If people with Down syndrome are unsuccessful, disability studies points the finger at inadequate resources, inflexible teaching strategies, and flawed standards for measuring accomplishment and worth. Instead of focusing on fixing individual defects, it calls for the resources to support people with disabilities in all aspects of life.

As I've watched Henry grow up, I've come to believe that his disability lies somewhere in between the two poles. He is certainly more successful in environments that accommodate many different ways of learning and behaving, but there is no environmental change that can erase his disability, which also has to do with differences of mind and body. That said, if Henry were offered a drug that could help him to better learn and adapt, would I take it? There is no easy answer to this question. I'll do anything possible to make sure Henry gets to lead a full and satisfying life. At the same time, I know drugs that affect brain function often have side effects that may be worse than the original symptoms they are designed to treat. If a drug to improve cognition made Henry stop being Henry in some fundamental way, then the answer is no.

On the night of Dr. Kinsella's talk, there was a feeling of urgency in the room. One parent spoke movingly to the small audience about how important it is for each of us to contribute to the cause of Down syndrome research. If not parents, then who? she asked. Down syndrome studies receive little funding from the National Institutes of Health and other government agencies because it is seen as a preventable condition. Scientists would much prefer to come up with safer ways of preventing genetically defective babies from being born than to work on improving the cognition of people living with Down syndrome. And so the very well-funded, very profitable race to develop earlier and less invasive prenatal tests to detect and eliminate fetuses with Down syndrome continues. In early 2012 the company Sequenom announced the MaterniT21 PLUS blood test, which could be administered to women as early in their pregnancy as ten weeks. In a press release, the company touts its commitment to providing "superior prenatal care," continuing the by now familiar conflation of maternal health with the genetic makeup of the fetus, as well as lumping Down syndrome together with such fatal conditions as Trisomies 13 and 18.

Ongoing social prejudice coexists uneasily with the increased visibility and acceptance of Down syndrome. Last summer, a California family splurged on first-class airplane tickets, only to be prevented from boarding because the pilot thought their teenage son with Down syndrome was a "flight risk." Despite their protests, they were escorted from the gate and rebooked on another flight, where they were assigned to the back of the plane. Stories like this might tempt us to focus on the injustice to the individuals involved, but it's important to remember that their experiences reflect systematic prejudice and misunderstanding. We all love heartwarming stories of success and accomplishment. But we're far from being a society that respects the rights of people with disabilities and their families, or that readily gives them the chance to flourish.

Even as I wrote about the invaluable, life-changing impact of early intervention, those programs were being eviscerated by budget cuts. The *New York Times* continues to publish articles on corrupt service providers who exploit the system for their own financial gain. While the dishonesty of those agencies should be exposed and punished, such stories only encourage the mistaken image of services for people with disabilities as a bloated and unnecessary drain on public coffers. When Henry was a baby, I was awed to discover the generosity and foresight of state-sponsored programs that make such a clear and immediate difference in the lives of children with disabilities. Every year the board of ed is more reluctant to assign the kinds of preschool services Henry received, which have been so essential to his development and future independence. As I watch such services being eroded from within, I worry that children just entering the system will be denied the same opportunities that Henry enjoyed. This is a misguided case of robbing Peter to pay Paul, since children who receive inadequate support in their early years will inevitably be more expensive and less independent later in life.

All of this gives me plenty to think about, and disability studies continues to be at the center of my intellectual world. The project that got off to such a shaky start has flourished, with a mailing list that now includes more than one hundred students, scholars, and supporters from throughout the region. I got the college to start a committee devoted to issues related to teaching students with disabilities, and faculty and staff have affirmed our efforts. Every year I teach at least one course on disability studies. It's gratifying to watch my students learning to think differently about justice, inclusion, accommodation, and dependency. I learn a great deal from them in return, as they challenge me to keep evolving along with the changes in the political, cultural, and scientific environment.

And the rest? I'm still alive. I just saw my doctor for my annual physical, where she pronounced me to be healthy and sound. We had our annual discussion about lung cancer, which, she reminded me, has only the slightest genetic component. Once again, she mentioned the option of the CT scan, which she would enable but not recommend. This time I didn't even take the prescription. Of course, after leaving her office I agonized for hours. But then I told myself, firmly, that enough was enough. I won't say I'm not tempted to call her back and tell her I've changed my mind. But I haven't.

THE THING ABOUT A TRUE STORY is that there is no obvious place to end. Literary critics will tell you that comedy ends in marriage, tragedy in death. But how many stories really end that way? Our story has no marriages, few deaths, no clear invitation to closure. And I hate goodbyes. I think my extreme separation anxiety must come from the fact that goodbyes always remind me of more permanent kinds of loss.

Unlike his mother, Henry has no problem with endings. He especially likes books that have the words "THE END" written on the last page. In their absence he is happy to announce the ending in a loud, decisive voice. To him, endings represent possibility. Why worry about coming to the end when there are always new books to read? Or the opportunity to start a favorite story all over again? I've made sure these two words always close the books I use for his literacy program. Unlike "see" and "love," he never gets them wrong. I like to think that someday Henry will read every word of this book, taking pleasure in seeing our entwined stories recorded in print. It will be some time before he gets there. And so, in the spirit of Henry, who clearly knows that endings are also always about new beginnings, I've decided to close this chapter of our story with the words I know he can read.

THE END.

Selected Bibliography

BOOKS AND ARTICLES

Adams, Rachel. *Sideshow U.S.A.: Freaks and the American Cultural Imagination.* Chicago: University of Chicago Press, 2001.

Andrews, Susanna. "Arthur Miller's Missing Act." *Vanity Fair,* September 2007. http://www.vanityfair.com/culture/features/2007/09/miller200709.

Antler, Joyce. "Progressive Education and the Scientific Study of the Child: An Analysis of the Bureau of Educational Experiments." *Teachers College Record* 83 (1982): 559–91.

Asch, Adrienne, and Eric Parens, eds. *Prenatal Testing and Disability Rights.* Washington, DC: Georgetown University Press, 2000.

Becker, Amy Julia. *A Good and Perfect Gift: Faith, Expectations, and a Little Girl Named Penny.* Roosevelt, NY: Bethany House, 2011.

Benda, Clemens. *Mongolism and Cretinism: A Study of the Clinical Manifestations and the General Pathology of Pituitary and Thyroid Deficiency.* New York: Grune and Stratton, 1946.

Bérubé, Michael. *Life as We Know It: A Father, a Family, and an Exceptional Child.* New York: Pantheon, 1996.

Bogdan, Robert. *Freak Show: Presenting Human Oddities for Amusement and Profit*. Chicago: University of Chicago Press, 1990.

Brousseau, Kate. *Mongolism: A Study of the Physical and Mental Characteristics of Mongolian Imbeciles*. Baltimore: Williams and Wilkins, 1928.

Cantu, Carolyn. "Early Intervention Services: A Family-Professional Partnership." *EP Magazine*, December 2002, 47–50.

Carey, Allison C. *On the Margins of Citizenship: Intellectual Disability and Civil Rights in Twentieth-Century America*. Philadelphia: Temple University Press, 2010.

Carlson, Licia. *The Faces of Intellectual Disability: Philosophical Reflections*. Bloomington: Indiana University Press, 2009.

Charon, Rita. *Narrative Medicine: Honoring the Stories of Illness*. New York: Oxford University Press, 2008.

Cunningham, Cliff. *Understanding Down Syndrome: An Introduction for Parents*. Cambridge, MA: Brookline, 1988.

Davis, Lennard, ed. *The Disability Studies Reader*. New York: Routledge, 2010.

———. *Enforcing Normalcy: Disability, Deafness, and the Body*. New York: Verso, 1995.

Down, John Langdon. *On Some of the Mental Affections of Childhood and Youth*. London: J. A. Churchill, 1887.

Fiedler, Leslie. *Freaks: Myths and Images of the Secret Self*. New York: Anchor, 1993.

Ginsberg, Faye, and Rayna Rapp. "Enabling Disability: Rewriting Kinship, Reimagining Citizenship." *Public Culture* 13 (2001): 533–56.

Goodey, C. F. *A History of Intelligence and Intellectual Disability: The Shaping of Psychology in Early Modern Europe*. Surrey: Ashgate, 2011.

Gould, Stephen Jay. *The Mismeasure of Man*. New York: Norton, 1996.

Grinberg, Jamie Gerardo Alberto. " 'I Had Never Been Exposed to Teaching Like That': Progressive Teacher Education at Bank Street During the 1930s." *Teachers College Record* 104 (2002): 1422–60.

Hurley, Dan. "A Drug for Down Syndrome." *New York Times Magazine*, July 29, 2011.

Kingsley, Jason, and Mitchell Levitz. *Count Us In: Growing Up with Down Syndrome*. New York: Harcourt Brace, 1994.

Kittay, Eva Feder. *Love's Labor: Essays on Women, Equality, and Dependency*. New York: Routledge, 1998.

Kumin, Libby. "Speech Intelligibility and Childhood Verbal Apraxia in Children with Down Syndrome." *Down Syndrome Research and Practice* 10 (2006): 10–22.

———. "You Said It Just Yesterday, Why Not Now? Developmental Apraxia of Speech in Children and Adults with Down Syndrome." *Disability Solutions* 5, no. 2 (2002): 1–15.

MacGregor, John M. *Metamorphosis: The Fiber Art of Judith Scott*. Oakland, CA: Creative Growth Art Center, 1999.

McCullers, Carson. *Member of the Wedding*. New York: Mariner, 2004.

Meza, James P., and Daniel S. Passerman. *Integrating Narrative Medicine and Evidence-Based Medicine: The Everyday Social Practice of Healing*. Bucks, UK: Radcliffe, 2011.

Millar, Diane C., Janice C. Light, and Ralf W. Schlosser. "The Impact of Augmentative and Alternative Communication Intervention on the Speech Production of Individuals with Developmental Disabilities: A Research Review." *Journal of Speech, Language, and Hearing Research* 49 (2006): 248–64.

Nussbaum, Martha. *Frontiers of Justice: Disability, Nationality, Species Membership*. Cambridge: Harvard University Press, 2006.

Olson, Carrie. "Lessons by Abigail: Educating a Seasoned Speech-Language Pathologist Named 'Mom.'" *Disability Solutions* 5, no. 3 (2003): 1–15.

Piepmeier, Alison. "Saints, Sages, and Victims: Endorsement of and Resistance to Cultural Stereotypes in Memoirs by Parents of Children with Disabilities." *Disability Studies Quarterly* 32, no. 1 (2012), http://dsq-sds.org/article/view/3031/3058.

Rapp, Rayna. *Testing Women, Testing the Fetus: The Social Impact of Amniocentesis in America*. New York: Routledge, 2000.

Rothman, Barbara Katz. *Genetic Maps and Human Imaginations: The Limits of Science in Understanding Who We Are*. New York: Norton, 1998.

Rothschild, Joan. *The Dream of the Perfect Child*. Bloomington: Indiana University Press, 2005.

Sandel, Michael. *The Case Against Perfection: Ethics in the Age of Genetic Engineering*. Cambridge: Belknap Press of Harvard University Press, 2009.

Shapiro, Joseph. *No Pity: People with Disabilities Forging a Civil Rights Movement*. New York: Times Books, 1993.

Siebers, Tobin. *Disability Aesthetics*. Ann Arbor: University of Michigan Press, 2010.

——. *Disability Theory*. Ann Arbor: University of Michigan Press, 2008.

Skotko, B. "Mothers of Children with Down Syndrome Reflect on Their Postnatal Support." *Pediatrics* 115 (2005): 64–77.

——. "Prenatally Diagnosed Down Syndrome: Mothers Who Continued Their Pregnancies Evaluate Their Health Care Providers." *American Journal of Obstetrics and Gynecology* 192 (2005): 670–77.

Skotko, B., G. Capone, and P. Kishnani for the Down Syndrome Diagnosis Study Group. "Postnatal Diagnosis of Down Syndrome: Synthesis of the Evidence on How Best to Deliver the News." *Pediatrics* 124 (2009): e751–58.

Skotko, B., P. Kishnani, and G. Capone for the Down Syndrome Diagnosis Study Group. "Prenatal Diagnosis of Down Syndrome: How Best to Deliver the News." *American Journal of Medical Genetics, Part A* 149 A (2009): 2361–67.

Skotko, Brian G., and Susan P. Levine. *Fasten Your Seatbelt: A Crash Course on Down Syndrome for Brothers and Sisters*. Bethesda, MD: Woodbine, 2009.

——. "Having a Brother or Sister with Down Syndrome: Perspectives from Siblings." *American Journal of Medical Genetics Part A* 155 (2011): 2348–59.

Skotko, Brian G., S. P. Levine, and R. Goldstein. "Having a Son or Daughter with Down Syndrome: Perspectives from Mothers and Fathers." *American Journal of Medical Genetics Part A* 155 (2011): 2335–47.

Smith, Phil, ed. *Whatever Happened to Inclusion?* New York: Peter Lang, 2009.

Stray-Gunderson, Karen. *Babies with Down Syndrome: A New Parents' Guide.* 2nd ed. Bethesda, MD: Woodbine, 1995.

Strohm, Kate. *Being the Other One: Growing Up with a Brother or Sister Who Has Special Needs.* Boston: Shambhala, 2005.

Thomson, Rosemarie Garland. *Staring: How We Look.* London: Oxford University Press, 2009.

Trent, James W. *Inventing the Feeble Mind: A History of Mental Retardation in the United States.* Berkeley: University of California Press, 1995.

Winzer, Margret. *The History of Special Education: From Isolation to Inclusion.* Washington, DC: Gallaudet University Press, 1993.

Wolstenholme, G. E. W., and Ruth Porter, eds. *Mongolism: In Commemoration of Dr. John Langdon Haydon Down.* London: Churchill, 1967.

FILMS

Down Syndrome: The First 18 Months. Dir. Will Schermerhorn. Blueberry Shoes Productions, 2003.

Girlfriend. Dir. Justin Lerner. Strand Releasing, 2012.

Including Samuel. Dir. Dan Habib. DH Photography, 2009.

Me Too (Yo También). Dir. Álvaro Pastor. Olive Films, 2011.

Praying with Lior. Dir. Ilana Trachtman. Ruby Pictures, 2007.

Think of Me First as a Person. Dir. George Ingmire and Dwight Core. Miabuelo Productions, 2006.

What's Under Your Hat? Dir. Lola Barrera and Iñaki Peñafiel. The Cinema Guild, 2007.

WEBSITES

Brian Skotko, MD, http://www.brianskotko.com/

Down Syndrome: Health Issues, http://www.ds-health.com/

Down Syndrome Education International, http://www.dseinternational .org/en/gb/

Down Syndrome Foundation of Orange County, http://dsfoc.org/

Down Syndrome Research and Treatment Foundation, http://www.dsrtf .org/

GiGi's Playhouse Down Syndrome Awareness Centers, http:// gigisplayhouse.org/

Michael Bérubé, http://www.michaelberube.com/

National Down Syndrome Congress, http://ndsccenter.org/

National Down Syndrome Society, http://www.ndss.org/

Riverbend Down Syndrome Association, http://www.riverbendds.org/ index.htm?page=home.html